Praise for
THE NEXT ACT

The system wants you to believe your shelf life has expired. It's waiting for you to shrink, to become invisible, to quietly fade away. Michael Feeley is here to help you see that this isn't true. Go, go, go.

—Seth Godin, Author of *This is Marketing*

The Next Act is a bold, honest, and deeply inspiring guide for anyone facing an unexpected career transition. Michael doesn't sugarcoat the fears and uncertainties of reinvention—he meets them head-on, offering wisdom, resilience, and a path forward. Through compelling personal stories and practical advice, he shows that career change isn't about starting over—it's about leveraging everything you've built to create a future that excites you. If you're wondering what's next, this book is the script you need to take control and step into your next act with confidence.

—Dr. Marshall Goldsmith, the *Thinkers50* #1 Executive Coach and New York Times bestselling author of *The Earned Life*, *Triggers*, and *What Got You Here Won't Get You There.*

The good news and the bad news are the same news. We are living longer now. It's good news if you have a job you love and friends, family, and a sweet dog by your side. It's bad news if you are stuck in a job you no longer love (or never did), recognize that you're in the fourth quarter of your life, and nothing calls to you. You are no longer a participant. You are a spectator trapped in a familiar cycle of unproductive thoughts with no idea where you're going. This is where Michael Feeley comes in with this fantastic, much-needed book, which will actually be helpful to anyone at any age. The writing is gorgeous, the questions are provocative, and the result is clarity about what you want, why you want it, and how to get it, including how to create a job out of thin air. This book has smarts plus heart. I loved it.

—Susan Scott, author of *Fierce Conversations: Achieving Success at Work and in Life – One Conversation at a Time; Fierce Leadership: A Bold Alternative to the Worst "Best" Practices in Business Today;* and *Fierce Love: Creating a Love That Lasts – One Conversation at a Time*

The Next Act removes the complexity, confusion, and fear of looking for new work and building your next career as a mature person. Consider it the blueprint for success distilled into easy, achievable steps that get results. This book is refreshing and empowering. A must-read.

—Chip Conley, Founder MEA and NY Times Bestselling Author

The Next Act is a guide for anyone with a dream that feels out of reach. Jargon-free, it is the least "coachy" book I've encountered on the subject. Feeley shares his experiences of reinventing himself professionally and personally, as well as examples of the journeys of some of his worldwide clients. He offers actionable exercises that can free you from where you are to where you dream to go. If you're feeling that tug to move on in your life but are stuck for myriad legitimate reasons such as fear, finances, other people's expectations, and self-confidence, if you've cringed at the word "coaching," this book is a must-read.

—Laura Meagher, Emmy Award-Winning Journalist and Personal Coach

The Next Act is an empowering guide for job seekers looking to translate their skills into tangible, performance-driven outcomes. Rather than focusing on outdated resumes and generic qualifications, Feeley provides a blueprint for leveraging transferable skills to meet real-world business challenges—exactly what hiring managers and recruiters seek. His approach aligns seamlessly with the performance-based hiring principles I advocate, helping professionals articulate their value through measurable achievements. If you're at a career crossroads, this book will help you craft a compelling career narrative that proves your ability to deliver results, making you a stronger, more confident job candidate.

—Lou Adler, CEO, Performance-Based Hiring Learning Systems and author of *Hire with Your Head* and *The Essential Guide to Hiring*

Wise people don't leave their future to chance. *The Next Act* is a heartfelt and practical guide to navigating mid-life and beyond career transitions with clarity and confidence. Michael Feeley

shares his own journey—from professional actor to recruiter to sought-after coach—bringing wisdom and depth to every page. The stories are moving, the exercises insightful, and the encouragement a balm for the soul of any job seeker. Now, you can step into your next role with renewed passion and purpose.
—Louise Karch, Award-winning author

Real-life advice for real-world dilemmas—here's the roadmap needed to live your best life!
—Angela Beeching, Arts Career Specialist and author of *Beyond Talent: Creating a Successful Career in Music*

The Next Act is a masterclass in reinvention. Michael reminds us that our skills, experiences, and aspirations don't have an expiration date—they are assets waiting for the right stage. This book is a must-read for anyone ready to step into their encore with clarity, confidence, and purpose.
—Scott Perry, Creative on Purpose

This gem of a book is woven with personal anecdotes and engaging stories, offering a wealth of practical, actionable advice. If you're asking yourself, "What comes next?" this book is a must-read. *The Next Act* is an essential guide for anyone ready to embrace change and take charge of their next act.
—LisaMarie Dias, Founder of LisaMarie Dias Designs

Life experience powers this book forward, as do the simple questions and exercises that help break down the obstacles that stop most people from moving forward and creating possibilities. I challenge you to read *The Next Act* and not embark on your next act!

—Zelda Gray, Retired Global Vice President of Human Resources, Mars Incorporated

The Next Act is brilliant. Michael uses his vast experience and intelligence to communicate practical, simple yet complex tools for foraying into a new career. He invites us to lean into our gifts and talents to find work that matters well into our golden years.

—Nadine Kelly, M.D., E-RYT, Health Integration Coach, Host of Health Raisers

For years, I sought advice for answers to my career challenges. While many books offered helpful advice, their perspectives were often limited to just one part of the elephant. *The Next Act* addresses the whole elephant—understanding that all business challenges are, at their core, personal ones. This book connects the dots between life and business, which is rare and invaluable. Readers, consider yourselves fortunate to have such hard-earned wisdom in printed form.

—Andrew Ingkavet, author, entrepreneur, composer, former MTV VJ, and founder of the Musicolor Method

The Next Act is a true reflection of Feeley's passion for empowering individuals to reinvent themselves and live a life driven by purpose. It contains practical strategies and an empowering and generous message. If you're ready to make a meaningful change, *The Next Act* is the perfect resource to guide you along the way. And if you think you are not ready yet, get the book too, as it also speaks to goal-setting and action broken down into smaller, manageable steps.

—Julien Fortuit, International Business and Career Coach

THE NEXT ACT

A COMPLETE GUIDE TO **CAREER CHANGE**, PROFESSIONAL REINVENTION, AND **FINDING WORK THAT MATTERS**

MICHAEL **FEELEY**

SUMMIT PRESS

Printed in the United States of America
First Printing, 2025
ISBN: 979-8-9852063-2-6
Library of Congress Number: 2025900132

Summit Press Publishers
P.O. Box 1356
Intervale, New Hampshire 03845

For information about special discounts available for bulk purchase, workshops, retreats, and webinars associated with this book or offered by Michael Feeley, please contact him at www.michaelfeeleylifecoach.com

*To everyone who yearns to
make their lives count, especially those
50 – 60 – 70 – 80+ years old
who have much more to give to
the world and wish to continue
living their dreams full out.*

*And . . . Thank you, Albert,
for believing in me and always
offering kindness, passion, and truth.*

Table of Contents

Part III: An Achievable Plan

Introduction

You thought you were set in this career and would retire at this company. But suddenly, they closed after you'd worked there for years . . . or spat you out . . . or put you next to the boiler room because someone more "gung-ho" entered the scene. You didn't see it coming, and now there's a giant, red neon sign flashing, "You're old. Out of a job. What the F$?# do you do now?"

An avalanche of fears comes crashing down. Suddenly, age is blaring at you; you've never experienced the subject of growing older in such an alarming, relevant, and weakening way before. You're vulnerable. *"How do I start over again?"* you ask yourself. *"Do I keep doing the same thing I'm doing now, having to prove myself again?"*

How do you switch careers late in life when you're 50, 60, or 70? The system, society, the culture, and the status quo want to limit you, to tell you that you've reached a certain age and it's time to go, to disappear. People will happily let you know you're slowing down and need to step down. You're not as sharp as you once were. You had your time, but that time is way behind you. Retire? What a word.

Maybe your biggest worry is making money. How will you support yourself and your family? The pressure can be overwhelming. If you're in mid-level management making a high salary, younger workers are likely moving in fast. That's intimidating. Maybe you're noticing how people dismiss and make less of your value and years of experience. *"I'm not* current," you might think. *"I don't have the tech skills, and companies are unwilling to* train." Then you really get nervous. *"Prepare for interviews when I haven't done that in* years?" The thought of it makes you sick to your stomach.

Many of the people I work with have lost sight of the possibilities and their potential when they find themselves at a career crossroads. Most humans are wildly more resourceful and resilient than they know. If they haven't been edged out, many of my clients feel trapped and deeply unappreciated in their present work. My job is to help them examine the options, to explore and exploit the unlimited possibilities they are too scared to see. Believe me, it's a new adventure studying yourself and your options.

I've helped countless people see that their skills and attitudes will lead them to new work opportunities, rebuild their vocation, and reinvent themselves by honoring all that they are. That means explicitly seeing and claiming the limitless value of their skills. I help people create positive change and live in a new and empowering way with job pride.

But I don't just understand your plight on a professional level; I've been there myself.

How I Know What You're Going Through

The Majestic Theatre on West 44th Street in New York City. "The Big League," better known as Broadway. Thirty years into my acting and singing career, there I was, auditioning for the title role in the musical *Phantom of the Opera*. I worked hard to get there; I'm talking about years of training and experience performing in various plays. Being a professional actor in New York City has been my heart's desire since I was eleven and saw my first musical. (Yes, I was that kid.)

A junior-high friend had an extra ticket to the high school musical *The Boy Friend* and asked if I wanted to go. When we got there, the auditorium was packed. People were talking and laughing in the lobby and the aisles. Lights flickered off and on, and we all began to take our seats. Down went the house lights, and the orchestra started to file in from the left. So many happy people dressed up and carrying instruments and sheet music, smiling, passing by the black baby grand piano, setting up behind music stands as people clapped for them.

When all was ready, the conductor tapped his wand—orchestra alert—and the Roaring Twenties Charleston music of the overture poured out. The sound was loud and thrilling. Suddenly, the dark green velvet curtains parted to the brilliant lights and colors of the set; an energetic, red-haired girl dashed in, darting around the stage. Others soon joined her, talking and laughing; they began to sing and dance wildly, free and open; then cheers of joy and applause from the audience exploded.

Right then, I knew that was what I wanted to do with my life: sing and act in musicals, entertain people, give others pleasure, and be alive and happy. This was my life purpose. I made a plan to build my dream career. It was filled with details, and I worked on it daily for years.

Over the years, I enjoyed incredible successes and landed dream parts. I loved the people I worked with. I learned from great directors, producers, actors, musicians, conductors, stage managers, agents, make-up artists, stylists, pianists, acting and singing teachers, and writers. I worked in famous theatres, for events, openings, and award ceremonies. I knew the thrill of performing live for an audience, that human connection—person to person—with an audience that had come to be entertained and moved. I could feel the pleasure and pain they took from the words and music of a play. That's the silver, gold, and platinum ring you go after as an actor and hold on to every time you perform. It's a privilege you earn, a precious treasure to protect in your hands and heart. And I was crazy for it all.

The audition, the one on West 44th, went well. I was proud of my work.

Then, the wait.

It's unusual to immediately hear if you got the part or are called back for more auditioning. The stakes are high, so that not knowing can feel all-encompassing. I vibrated with this chance and the outcome. *"The phone will ring at any second!"* While excruciating, I felt the immense hope of winning alongside the fear I'd be passed by. Often, you never hear, and the passing of time and no one calling is cruel. Fortunately, I had an agent. Two days later, he called with the news that I didn't get the part. Supportive, he promised more auditions of this caliber.

I hung up and collapsed, worn out. Seldom do you know why you weren't chosen. You have no recourse for what to work on to improve. Rejection is always crushing because you want to work at what you love best. And that role was an outstanding opportunity that would propel me to the next big promotion, stardom on Broadway. Though I felt massive disappointment, I held on to the positives: I was asked to audition; people saw value in me; they heard me sing and act. I was a contender. I had the goods to play this part and others—the skills, the looks, solid experience, and a top agent who believed in me. That's how I countered the rejection. Not by beating myself up and cursing the world for not coming through for me, but with the truth as I saw it and a good deal of gratitude. You bet it takes time to adjust, heal, and regroup from loss and letdown. But you do. It's part of the job and the journey you sign up for when you choose to be an actor.

Ready to gamble, to throw the dice and hope to win, that was *Phantom*. Even though I didn't win the jackpot, I wasn't broke. So, to end the adventure that I chose and built—to end the roller-coaster ride, the vocation of heartfelt love—was big.

It was a turning point. I was smart enough to see I was at a dead end. I could keep going and deal with the cards I was holding, but I wasn't about to end up a spear carrier at the Met.

There's nothing wrong with that choice, but I wanted to leave on a glorious high note, with the dignity I had established, and not fade away from all I had built.

"Do I keep grinding away, waiting for these few exciting opportunities to come up for me, or end my beloved acting career and do something else?" That's the question I asked myself. Was it time to turn around and drive in a completely new direction?

One minute, I would think, *"My God! End . . . stop . . . finish . . . quit . . . do something else?"* I never expected to be thinking this. Not performing? No more auditioning? No more singing and acting lessons? Acting *was* my entire life.

The next minute, I would consider the fact that I needed to work. Yes, Broadway had been the dream, but I went wherever the work was—always had.

For a while, I made career choices to stay and work in New York, auditioning for commercials and soaps and being selected into an elite circle working as a Ford model. I worked all kinds of other jobs simultaneously to make a living. I was willing to remain in the city, in my career, to see if I could make it work for me, at least for a while longer. Acting had never been about the money. It was about art, living in art. Being alive. To be ready for a theater gig that might come my way, I remained prepared, well-trained, and studied, finely tuning the skills that I was proud of.

Because what was the alternative? Build another career after I'd poured everything into this work I loved. Loved. What could I do that I loved—teach? The very idea did nothing for me. Anyway, I didn't have the skills to teach, not really.

Patching my acting career together worked for a while, until it didn't. I would need to pursue something else if I wanted any kind of life.

Then, the fear kicked in. Fear of change. Fear of the unknown. Fear I'd become a nobody. A has-been. A failure.

"Should I go or should I stay?" I didn't know. After all, where else would I ever find as much meaning and happiness as I did in acting? Where would I find the opportunity to profoundly impact and contribute to other people's lives? What purpose would I serve? Who was going to hire an aging actor? Who was going to take me seriously? Maybe giving up on my dream was me selling out and betraying the most profound thing in me. I paused and really felt the gut punch. I knew what my friends would say. "So, you finally quit. We've been wondering when you would." Friends? People mean well but often lack the compassion you are desperately hoping for.

The Next Act

The essence and meaning of me, Michael Feeley, was acting and singing. I was at my best, most alive, and expressed doing that. What would I replace that with?

Yet, I started looking for my next act. I began to ask myself: *"What do I want to do? What do I like? Where could I make a living fast? Where could I feel useful? Where would I be appreciated and a success?"*

This choice to change careers was traumatic, emotionally and physically distressing. A new career did not magically materialize the moment I said "stop" to the old career. I had to learn how to move into a new mindset and heartset. Daily routines and processes, business direction, and commitments all had to be replaced—but replaced with what? I had little idea.

Then I took solace; I had worked all kinds of jobs. When the play finished, I had to find work until I found a new role. For a while, I sold cruises for an international cruise corporation— and I was good at it. So, as I pounded the pavement and the taxi horns blared, it occurred to me that a customer service job was a possibility.

Days later, I applied for a job, but for some reason, the owner of the staffing agency didn't send me on the interview but wanted to train me in personnel—to interview people and fill jobs. I'm a people person, so it sounded easy and fun. Soon, I filled jobs and offered top service to clients and candidates. I found myself thriving in this industry and moved into outside sales and client development at other staffing firms.

There was a definite connection to acting. It was akin to being onstage and rehearsing scene work as I met people to find them jobs. I studied them and their resumes as I would a character in a play. I coached them, like a director, as we worked on preparing for interviews and getting a job. I wouldn't have seen the natural bridge between careers had I not tried my hand at the job.

But like any play, there was more than a single act. At fifty-eight, I unexpectedly lost my thirteen-year job as a headhunter due to downsizing. One day, I was employed; the next, unemployed. I panicked. I was too old to start over again and needed to make money.

A dear friend dragged me to Starbucks and asked what I planned to do. I had no idea. I could stay in corporate America working for other staffing firms, but I didn't want to. I had to break away from the relentless stress burning me out and making me constantly angry. I was tired of not being promoted; my worth was judged continuously on numbers and the money I brought in. Here I was working with humanity—finding people jobs, caring about others, building incredible business relationships—but all that seemed to matter to my bosses was the almighty dollar.

My friend suggested life coaching, which I knew nothing about. After researching the role, the connection with my years of recruiting and placing people in jobs was immediate. I realized a career and life coach was the way for me to go. I returned to school and got certified as a professional coach, which was the best choice I ever made. The training added to my skills, and I discovered new depth and self-expression.

What I now experience coaching others far surpasses what I felt acting on a stage. It's priceless, deeper, and more rewarding than I expected.

And it all came out of the adversity of losing a job.

So, what will be your next act? Because if there's one thing I've learned, it's this: all your skills are transferable. All your training, education, and experience in any industry are valuable and highly useful. Don't let anyone tell you otherwise. You don't have to dumb them down or sell yourself short. You are qualified. Your present credentials will work in other places. Once you see your value, you can pivot into a new line of work with confidence, pride, and success. Once you recognize your transferable skills and value, it's possible to better your current work environment if you choose to stay. You are not stuck; you have choices.

The Answers Are Within

The questions I pose to my clients and the lessons I share are the very ones you'll discover in the pages ahead. This book will guide you toward finding the answers that live in you—to break up blocks, limiting beliefs, and faulty assumptions. It will be your catalyst for change. It will take you from where you are to where you want to be, creating remarkable and sustainable results. You can also access additional resources at michaelfeeleylifecoach.com/bonus.

If you're at a career crossroads, it's time to explore if your present work will take you where you want to go or if it's time to move on to other job options. It's time to consider the big, overarching questions:

- How do you know if it's time for a change, even if you feel trapped because you don't know where to start?

- How do you make a change with dignity and in such a way that works?

- How do you keep your present job and look for something new?

- How do you reinvent your career in your fifties, sixties, and beyond?

- What do you do when the resume and interview process has changed—when it doesn't honor your skills and potential, often feels unkind, and causes you to lose faith that change is possible?

- What if you don't want to start over and lose everything you've already built and have?

- Is it time to retire or just quit or reinvent yourself?

- Should you bear your troubles and stick it out where you are? How do you change and tolerate a job you've outgrown or even hate?

- How do you deal with all the fears that accompany a potential job or career change?

- How do you track and manage all the moving pieces associated with applying for jobs or changing careers?

- How do you stay motivated if a change doesn't happen as quickly as you'd like?

Beyond hope, this book will provide you with the strategy and tools to enable you to stay on your feet and prosper, keep you healthy in body, mind, and spirit, set new goals and intentions, and act upon them, and replace your fears with confidence, truth, and meaningful work.

You have achieved things: promotions, recognition, awards, and respect. Work is a prominent part of your identity. It's who you are, and you don't need to suffer and downgrade to your industry's version of spear carrier. You're still valuable and probably more valuable than you realize.

Life is about building, honing, and applying your skills. The knowledge and wisdom you have are remarkable—and marketable. They make you who you are, enabling you to stand out and succeed. It's not the job or situation, title, or location of your office. It's showing up and claiming what you want, have earned, and deserve.

Let this next stage of your life be your encore, knowing that you're entitled to as many encores as you like . . .

PART I:
TAKING STOCK

1

You've Got Transferable Goods

It's possible to fly without motors, but not without knowledge and skill.
—Wilbur Wright

I walked away from acting with an abundance of advantageous skills and knew I could do it again in a new career once the initial shock wore off. You can, too. You can land solidly on your feet. You don't need to cower. There's no need to panic. You're not close to being done. You haven't finished your run. You're a player. Get off the bench and get back into the game.

It's not simply a matter of career moves. It's about developing self-confidence in your abilities and refusing to take no for an answer. If there's one thing I learned in acting, it's never taking no at face value. This practice will benefit you like no other. You'll want to spin into success, negotiate, and bargain right on the spot by connecting with the decision-maker.

It's about knowing who you are—a survivor. You're not someone to be tapped out, cut in front of, or put aside. It's a shift in mindset from too old to ever-so-valuable, desired, sought after—an asset and benefit for any company to hire you. You're in demand because of your skills and experience. You have integrity and status and a resume of detailed facts.

This mindset can connect you to your skills, the stuff you're truly good at—the things you love that allow you to live on your terms. With that, you'll never be stuck. You can work anywhere, rise in the ranks, or transition to your next dream. You can walk tall and proud and wow your audience.

It can guide your interviews. They're simply conversations, so you can talk your way into your new career with a rundown of your skills.

More importantly, it can feed a foundational belief in yourself that no one can shake, no matter how often they say no. It's the solid internal vision and appreciation of yourself that leads, connects, and makes things happen. It provides the confidence to let people know you're it. Nobody else will do.

Where It Starts

What are your skills and values? While related, there is a difference between the two.

Skills are the tools (abilities, knowledge) you use to achieve your goals. They may include multiple languages, organization, networking, team building, and listening; technology, mathematics, drawing, singing, architecture, sales, and writing—even running a marathon. For example, my most valuable skills are helping people get results, organization, and problem-solving.

Values are the ethical choices and personal beliefs that affect one's behavior and how one lives and treats others. They may include respect, kindness, gratitude, diversity, creativity, reliability, goodwill, courage, justice, curiosity, passion, forgiveness, honesty, positivity, trustworthiness, truth, and empathy.

As an aside, empathy is not the same as sympathy, which has pity to it. Empathy is a deeper connection; it's the ability and courage to stand in someone else's shoes, even if they are far different from you, with the intent to truly know them. It's what we each want as human beings: to be understood, to know that someone genuinely cares for us and sees our needs and wants, fears and worries, successes and dreams. When you have empathy for other human beings, they often respond with gratitude and relief. Their subsequent openness is something to cherish. Caring enough to go there, yup, another skill.

Personally, I would describe service and empathy as my core values.

You'll notice my examples include the "most valuable" skills and my "core" values. That's because there are varying degrees of both. You may be competent in some skills and excel in others; you may value many things, but some are an intrinsic part of who you are. All can be used to your advantage.

Furthermore, both skills and values are choices and actions. You can practice and improve your skills and practice and improve the integrity of your life and what you stand for, giving you the confidence and humility to say, "This is who I am; this is how I live my life." But first, you must know what they are and sufficiently respect them.

Here's how my skills and values worked together to help me transition from one career to another:

As with any audition, I was perfectly at ease selling myself and my services, setting up interviews, stepping onto new stages (so to speak), and doing all I could to convince a client that I was the best choice to find them qualified people for their jobs. I knew I'd come through for them, and I usually did.

Much like my character study work as an actor, I screened candidates and met with HR directors and CEOs, intensely aware of their feelings and what they were after. It helped me create a plan to help each person involved achieve their goals. Again, it was a skill and something I did with seriousness and integrity. It wasn't a game.

I was good at persuading people to meet with me and improvising on the spot.

Improvisation—the art of spontaneity, where you're given a situation that is unprepared and unrehearsed and required to come up with some response. It's an art in which actors must excel. This means that I was never stilted or dependent upon a script. I was natural, friendly, and genuinely engaged.

It also meant I was a good listener, which allowed me to tally the facts, zero in on the need, know when to move in or hold off, make suggestions, and create precise, caring results with the precision of a laser surgeon.

Like a scene in a play—watching, listening, working with others, and sincerely reacting—but it was recruiting and sales, with profitable results. I was a leading man in the theatre and continued to lead with my whole self, using all my tools and expertise in this new industry.

Understanding your core values before you consider your next career chapter will allow you to own yourself and identify opportunities best suited to you. You have to know what works for you and what doesn't. This is so important (and why I devoted an entire chapter to the subject).

List Your Transferable Goods

Before you consider entering the job market (or staying and improving on your current situation), you'll need to create a skill list. (Check out the bonus resource, "What Do You Do Better Than Anyone on the Face of the Earth?" at michaelfeeleylife-coach.com/bonus.)

Since it's a crucial step, make it real by writing it down in detail. I want you to honor and value yourself—Val-You. Sure, that's wordplay, but I'm deeply serious. Your skills create value for you and others. By value, I mean marketable currency. Skills are your assets. If you change jobs or professions, they make you stand out in your career.

I'm not talking about your role or job title, whether you have a corner office or a small cube facing a wall. I'm talking about what you have learned and what you worked hard to master.

Your ability, training, knowledge, and life experience are not just assets but your gold. They are what you have earned over the years, and they are resilient to change. You don't lose these things even if you move into another career. They are yours to carry and promote. They are not just tools; they are part of your identity; they make you shine, which will attract people and opportunities.

It's also important to note your talents. You may have been born with them, but they're often unreliable and temporary gifts. Raw and unshaped, they need to be cultivated, understood, and made durable through study and practice. Please don't take them for granted. Write them down, and then continue to show them love. If you commit to them for the rest of your life, you can create lasting strength and beauty by converting them into skills.

Create Your Life Resume

If you're mature (once disrespectfully known in staffing as "high mileage"), the thought of writing a resume—especially if you haven't had to write one for decades—may be met with ridicule.

Write a resume? One or two pages describing who I am, with dates? You've got to be kidding me. I'll end up stocking shelves at Walmart, cleaning apartments, or being a host at an aging residence complex with no pension.

Nothing is wrong with any of those jobs, mind you, but chances are good; there's more you're after and more you have to give.

The world opens up when you know what you're good at, how you excel, and what employers hunger for but cannot find. So, once you've written down your skills, you'll want to create your Life Resume.

Your Life Resume is a document that requires you to tell the truth (the whole truth and nothing but the truth) about who you are and what you do. It's where you list all the facts about your life relevant to your talents, learning, and life experiences. It explains your story and enables you to say, "This is who I am. This is what I do."

I'll be giving you plenty of exercises soon enough, but for now...consider what you might list under each bullet point statement:

- These are my core values.
- These are my gifts and talents.
- These are my skills.
- I do this better than anyone else on the face of the earth.
- These are my dreams. (More on this in another chapter.)

Your answers will help expand your resume (which we'll describe in detail in Chapter 16) beyond the standard one to two pages. Furthermore, it will enable you to clearly see how much you know and what you have to offer.

Discernment

The goal is to know what you have—your expertise, what works for you, where you excel, what gets you by, and what you should avoid. There's wisdom and power in discernment. You don't suddenly switch to football when your forte is the high dive. You need to know your 'SELF'—with a focus on sincerity over pretense, reality over unrealistic dreams.

Let's go one step deeper: your unique worth, which is also your potential, includes the contributions you made in your career—and what you hope to contribute. Consider the difference you hope to make in your own life, the lives of others, and even the world.

- What is your value as you see it?
- What do you offer people that is helpful to their lives?

When you do the work, you may be surprised to discover the abilities you have. For example, let's say you're a fantastic organizer. You could organize a paperclip and make it work better than it already does (and that's saying a lot because a paperclip is perfect in its simplicity and efficiency). If you're used to doing it without much thought, you may take it for granted and not consider it a master skill. But you'll discover much more meaning when you stop and look at what you do differently.

Your skills are the aces in your pocket, so why wouldn't you be completely sure of your market value? With this knowledge, you can talk your way into the next steps of your new career (or make the one you currently have that much better).

Knowing your market value—what's scarce and how you can fill it and even make it overflow—is key. Knowing will prevent you from making poor choices because you're too busy selling yourself to others and proving your worth.

It's Time to Act

As you begin this career change process, be kind to yourself. You are not alone in your fears. You may have questions, but those questions have answers.

The important thing is you value yourself. Under no circumstances are you to sell yourself short; sliding to the bottom is not allowed. It's strictly prohibited. Never cheapen your capabilities and think you must take a mediocre job.

Keep your vision of succeeding and being full of energy at the forefront. Trust yourself. You can find opportunities. You can also create opportunities. Decide where you want to go, and the chances are good you'll go further than expected.

One thing I know for sure is that you always have choices, especially when reinventing yourself, which is exciting stuff to work and play with. You can leave a used-up job or do something to make it far more palatable; pick yourself up off the floor if you get downsized or transition into a new career on your own. Every bit of your life is valuable and incredibly useful in your future work. It's there, waiting for you. You've just got to act. When you do... Hello encore, new purpose, new life.

2

Know Your Core Values

———

Everything can be taken from a man, but one thing: the last of
human freedoms—to choose one's attitude in any given
set of circumstances, to choose one's own way.

—Viktor Frankl

Maybe you've long believed you should bloom where you're planted—that you should be able to find happiness regardless of the environment or the circumstances. But that's not true. You bloom in the right kind of soil, and that soil is different for everyone.

If you want to be happy going to work, you'll probably want to be around those with similar characteristics and values—people who think and operate like you do. Because there's nothing worse than being a square peg in a round hole. You need to be in a culture where you can thrive, not simply survive.

You must know and be committed to your core values because standing by them can come with costs. Sometimes, your values will require you to turn away from a job or a job opportunity. You must know what you stand for to make the right choice, or you could lose your soul.

Case in point...

I was up for a part in a hot Off-Broadway production that was going on tour and then returning to Broadway with the promise of a movie. An agent set up a meeting with the producer/casting director. It was big. I was picking roles, promoting myself, and getting closer to realizing my dream of being a successful actor and singer. That person could help make that happen.

We sat in the hotel lobby as he told me about the show, his work, his vision, and why I was right for two of the roles. This was it; the next step in making a name for myself! Then he said, "I've told you what I can do for you. Now, let's go upstairs and see what you can do for me."

It was unfathomable. He had to be joking. I just stared at him. He was not joking. My dream did not include physical blackmail. He could help me get what I desperately wanted and worked my ass off for, but he wanted something cheap and lowdown in return. And let's face it, New York City is a big place, but people know who you are in the theatre, how you're progressing, and who you're studying with and sleeping with.

Not to mention, there was no guarantee that if I had sex with him, I would get the part. No guarantee I'd last through rehearsals. And people would know what I had done. I wanted to smash him in the face. *How could he do this?* What crappy power he held over me.

From somewhere outside of my body, I watched myself stand up, shaking with anger. "Please let me know about the audition. Thank you." Then, I turned and walked out.

There it was; the dark underbelly of art. I had heard stories but never imagined it would happen to me. When I told some of my friends, they said, "Are you crazy? This is your chance. It's just sex."

Time passed. I didn't get an audition.

That day, I learned that I had two choices: maintain my self-respect and integrity, my intent to honor art and myself, or comply and give in to the command of someone who wanted to control and break me, to own me for a little while. No matter how tempting the bargain was, I wasn't willing to roll in the gutter with that unprofessional slug.

Plenty of devils are ready to play on your vulnerability with little care for you. Their desire is simply to manipulate, bully, and use you for their gain. It's never worth it to lessen yourself and the respect you put into your work. You want—you need—to hold out for those beautiful, ethical opportunities that will also come along... if only you refuse to sell yourself out.

What Do You Stand For?

You likely have an inborn ethical desire to be just and to treat people fairly and respectfully. From there, you learn values by living in the world—from family, friends, school, culture, and society.

There are two kinds of values: **fear-based** and **conscious-based**.

Fear-based values hinder action because you want to avoid something. Conscious-based values help you take action because it's something you want to do, something you're passionate about. We judge ourselves on our ethical choices—the actions that we take and the actions that we avoid.

Whether fear-based or conscious-based, your values direct what you stand for and how you make choices: yes—no—I will—I won't—I can—I can't. Therefore, it's essential to be aware of the two—how they impact your ability to be true (or false) to yourself and make moral judgments about the world around you.

They can also change as you change and grow. Much like skills, you build your values by trying them out: does it stay true to me; does it fit my life personally and professionally; does it make me proud of the way I think and act? This "practice" is essential because your values reveal your attitude to the world.

The Core of Your Values

Most people have three to four core values. But there tends to be one that stands out. It's the one thing that is central to your existence or character. As such, it must be intertwined into everything you value. The core value I need to embody and be around is integrity. It's about personal honor. It's about being whole and true to myself in everything I do, even if no one is watching.

I suggest the same for you.

Integrity can be defined as "the quality of being honest and having strong moral principles... the state of being whole and undivided." It may also be defined as doing what is right for you—living free and happy—while not hurting others. It's leading your life the way you want, without judgment but with honor, valor, and love. It's facing things with wonder, understanding, and kindness.

Chances are good that you have an ethical unconscious that lets you know if you have been true to yourself and others. It's your inner compass of truth. (Don't forget that bonus content at michaelfeeleylifecoach.com/bonus; look for the resource titled "What is Being True to Yourself?")

When you set a high standard of integrity for yourself in all that you do, there are no half-assed attempts. You don't look for (or even want) things to be handed to you because you are committed to quality and distinction.

Now, I feel the need to touch on the fact that this commitment does not mean you work yourself to death or that you never ask for help. Again, integrity involves being true to yourself while not hurting others. When you try to do it all and burn yourself out, you not only hurt yourself but those around you as well. So, you do need to learn to pace yourself—to detach in the right ways—to recognize how all things work together.

Speaking of which, both integrity and integration come from the Latin word "integrare," which means "to make whole." Some people are different when they're home with their family than when they're at work or with strangers. There's no room for such things if you are truly living with integrity. You're whole. At all times and in all places.

It's not always easy. It may even make some uncomfortable (because of their lack of integrity). But it's worth it. So, keep your eyes on what's important and what's intrinsic.

And remember: integrity is persistence—steadiness—strength—reliability—confidence—freedom. It will guide your choices to do the right things and help others without personal or artistic betrayal. Integrity is your good name and honor—shouldn't that matter most to you?

Exercise: Consider Your Values

If you're wondering about your values and whether you're living and working in alignment with them, answer the following questions:

1. Why do your values matter to you?

2. How are your values working for you?

3. How do your values inspire respect?

4. Where might you compromise your values?

5. When life is good, what values are present and honored?

6. When life challenges you, what values might be in question?

Now, if you're wondering if you're acting with integrity because of all you stand to lose, here's an exercise I often have my coaching clients do (particularly when trying to describe why they're unhappy with their current job).

Exercise: How Do People Describe You?

Take a piece of paper and divide it into three columns.

Column 1 – Intimates

Column 2 – Friends/Co-workers

Column 3 – Strangers

In a simple word or two, list how people see you, such as friendly, hard-working, loyal, dull, always late, positive, caring, or creative.

When finished, ask yourself:

1. Are all three columns the same or different?

2. Am I the same person to everyone?

How much does it matter to you that you are one way wherever you go and whatever you do—that you're whole?

Since living on your own terms and being wholly faithful to your values is so important, I ask my clients to complete this exercise as well...

Exercise: When True to Yourself...

Answer the following questions:

1. What does it feel like when you live with integrity and are true to yourself?

   (I'm happy, calm, energized, focused, organized, grateful, clear, and not rushed. I feel peace, joy, and freedom, and well connected to other people and the world; my needs are minimal.)

2. What does it feel like when you live out of integrity and are not true to yourself?

   (I'm irritated, speedy, dull, nit-picky of other people and things, distracted, scattered, frustrated, tired, isolated, focused too much on me, things don't blend, I feel I'm missing out and lacking things. I feel shame because this is not me.)

   Study what you're doing in each state. Where, how, and why are you in or out of integrity? Knowing these things is important because living in or out of integrity will affect the quality of your life.

3. What are some of your core values that are deal breakers? What must you see around you to feel comfortable and valued?

   (Freedom, kindness, community, family, creativity, self-expression, growth, friendship...)

Always remember, you get to choose. You are never stuck. You get to leave a job, turn down a "golden opportunity," or say no to something that makes others think you are crazy. No matter what, your next chapter should reflect your value system. That's what will allow you to feel good about yourself and your decisions.

3

Reconnect With Your Dreams

———

"We are such stuff as dreams are made on."

—William Shakespeare

Let's work on reconnecting with your dreams.

But what is the stuff of dreams?

It may be:

Imagination, plans, strategies, and feelings

Belief in yourself and the world coming through for you

Passion, art, creativity, heart

Service and giving

Guts, drive, ambition, daring, wildness

Empathy, hope, wishes, generosity, heartache, gratitude, optimism

Clues, signals, signs, flags, flares, messages from the universe, the gods, and the angels

Connection with people

Collaboration

Previews of your future achievements

Dreams are meant to guide your life choices and capture your purpose. The things you dream about, desire, and vividly imagine are crucial because they represent who you are and what you are meant to do with your life here on Earth. Dreams are real things. They're the DNA, the building blocks of your life. You are entirely yourself with your dreams and hardly anything without them.

Your dreams are also a commitment. They are not meant to hang in the ether but to inspire action: a life direction, work goal, reason for building skills, and career choice. Gloria Steinem says, "Without leaps of imagination or dreaming, we lose the excitement of possibilities. Dreaming, after all, is a form of planning."

We're always dreaming—creating, imagining, planning, and plotting—or at least we should be. Your dreams should keep you up late at night and pull you out of bed way too early in the morning.

Some dreams are long-term; however, they take time to achieve, such as building a particular career where you study and practice skills. Other dreams are immediate, like suddenly finding the right teacher, suit, gift, or peach-colored rose bush for your garden.

You also dream when you sleep (whether you remember them or not). Such dreams often contain things you hope for and things to learn from; they may contain criticisms of yourself and others. They reveal what's happening in your subconscious, driving your actions throughout the day.

Some people (particularly those who are unhappy) say dreams are for fools. I disagree. Dreams are reality waiting for you to do the work and make them happen. They're meant to take you on the hero's journey. As with any great adventure, it will include joys and "sloggin' through hell" (in the words of the famous depression song, "Brother, Can You Spare a Dime?").

There are no guarantees you'll succeed when you venture forward. There's uncertainty and risk.

It might not work; you'll quite possibly fail, but you're committed to the journey. That's the crucial step—the commitment: *I'll do whatever it takes; I'm all in; nothing will stop me. Nothing!*

The journey will change you, and hopefully for the better. It will help you learn more about who you are and how you're stronger than you think; it will fill up your imagination and push your desire to succeed at the work that you love.

Your dreams matter.

Your Relationship with Your Dreams

Perhaps you're living your dream. If so, that's fantastic. Congratulations.

Your dreams may have driven you to design buildings, address the UN as a foreign dignitary, teach opera, design clothes, clean pools, manage properties, or offer a service that wows people because it meets their needs and aspirations. Perhaps they pushed you, with the crazy passion that accompanies dreams, to become a doctor, lawyer, or parent.

I often think of those who had a dream and did something about it in various occupations and at different ages. They devoted their lives to their vision. They wholeheartedly pursued their passion for history, art, fundraising, culture, politics, or social justice. Real people who went after a dream, not just for themselves but for humanity.

Perhaps you're returning to a dream because suddenly it's back in town, it's the right time, and you want to try to achieve it. *Why not?!* It might be writing, acting, singing, raising a family, teaching, traveling the world, being an IT wizard, running a Bed & Breakfast, living on an island in the Caribbean, or running your own company.

Or perhaps something pops up; you're fifty, sixty, seventy, or older, and you have a brand-new dream—something you really want.

Sometimes, you're driven to achieve a dream, regardless of age or season of life. Other times, you don't believe enough in yourself to follow the dream, so you release it, put it away, or (God forbid) give up! Even worse, you may be tempted to forget it ever existed in the first place. Whatever you do, don't do that. Do not give up.

The Problem with Dreams

Some people have a hard time with the word dream. They doubt. They limit themselves to prevent potential failure and disappointment; they block themselves from their heart's yearning.

Some find the word unrealistic. To them, it's fluff, pie in the sky, a pipe dream, fantasy—little more than a Disney cartoon with little Jiminy Cricket wishing on a star.

The fact is, we all have dreams. We all have something in our heads and hearts that we can't shake loose. You included. You may not tell people about your dream for fear they'll laugh and burst that precious bubble, but it's there.

So, use a different word:

Aspiration may be easier to live with

Goal sounds solid and normal

Purpose in life

Intention

Work you want to do, are interested in, and like

Whatever you call it, it's still powerful stuff. There's hunger in it. It includes real drive and (here it comes, the one that's overused and terrifying) passion.

Why is passion so scary? Because passion runs you. It's not something you can control. It's something that matters more to you than anything else in the world. You love and need it. And somewhere deep down inside, you're terrified it won't become a reality.

But let's look at this dream thing square in the eye. Let's plunge deeper into the heart of the matter by doing a little exercise.

Exercise: Fear Busting

What scares you most about going after your dream—
do you know? Speak it now and write it down so you can
hear it and see it:

I'm afraid _____

I believe the fears we each have (as we dream away) can include the fear of failure, success, or not trying (related to not starting—not acting), which may be the greatest fear of all. Think about it:

How scary is it not to try?

How heartbreaking is it not to act on your dreams?

The unknown can be frightening but also enticing. How can you let the allure of the unknown lead you into positive change instead of freezing you with fear?

Don't let your dream become an unlived choice that quickly and painfully changes into an unlived life.

People will criticize your dreams carelessly, maybe dismissing them with cold silence, but you can get through careless insults, fear, and shame by knowing yourself as thoroughly as possible and taking excellent care of what you're going after. This is your life, not other people's. Live your life for yourself.

I often felt my closest friends didn't take my dreams of singing and acting seriously. They thought I couldn't cut it, that I wasn't being sensible. When I poured out my heartfelt yearnings to them, they stared back, silent. I'd tell them of my successes, the prominent people I was auditioning for, the roles I was up for—many of which were for Broadway musicals—they'd tell me not to count on it. I hadn't paid my dues; I didn't have a name. Thankfully, I recognized they were likely waiting for me to cave in and quit the dream as many of them had done. All the naysayers didn't derail or smother the dream I was after.

To shield yourself against such criticism, consider why your dreams matter to you. Work through this exercise to connect with that...

Exercise: Your Dream Matters

Back to answering those key questions...

1. Why does this specific dream of yours matter?
2. What will it do for you once you achieve your dream?
3. How faithful are you to your dream? (Are you playing around? Cheating? Not committing fully for some reason?)

Note: Even if it's the "wrong" dream, consider it carefully and pursue it again with a fresh spirit. See your dream with new eyes. Reset it. Explicitly describe it. Any time is the best time to remember, renew, and realize your dreams, but now would be smart.

What a waste of time to simply think about your dreams, letting fear and doubt hold you back from acting on them and making them a reality. Have courage and believe in the possibilities and potential of your dreams.

Your dreams are worth it; they always have been.

Dreams Can Be Flexible

If you've given up on your dream, and I fervently hope with all my heart you have not, I beg you to act right now and reconnect with your dream. And remember, dreams are flexible. The essence remains the same, but how it looks may change over time. It's never too late to begin again. Change into your dreams. Make your life count the way you imagine, even if that means changing your job and establishing a new career.

I've worked with people who spent their lives studying music, singing, and playing instruments; those who ran schools, taught performance, and worked as executives and personal assistants. Now, they work in publicity and other high-level jobs, booking talent and scheduling concerts for symphony orchestras, ballet companies, and art galleries; they're writing professionally. Their dream of performance changed, but their connection to that dream, to art, still matters. Their dreams morphed into what is possibly a better way to express themselves, much like my move from acting to headhunting and coaching.

I've also worked with people who easily shifted from established careers in finance into advertising and publishing.

Then, there are those who want to be reporters and newscasters. They take related jobs that utilize their skills and imagination to prove themselves and establish their value. They know their abilities and let them shine every day—and they wound up getting what they wanted.

There are so many more...

People who dreamed of being movie stars, and they made it.

People who dreamed of living and working in New York City and Paris now do.

People who longed to be a pilot, and they're flying.

People who had a lifelong dream of studying and working with specific people, and they made it happen.

All real dreams. All possible.

What they all have in common is action. They acted on their dreams, wishes, desires, aspirations, hunger, yearnings, passions, and loves. They were flexible with the form their dreams took until they landed in the right spot.

How to Make Your Dreams Come True

Your dreams might be about your career, family, relationships, and lifestyle. Study them and let them guide you directly to the life you are meant to live.

What does it take to get there?

- A passionate belief in yourself and your abilities

- Trust that the world is on your side

- A solid strategic plan to achieve your dreams

- Guts, stamina, gratitude, and courage to pursue them

- Love, commitment, and some damn hard dream work

Give yourself the green light. You must believe in your dream and your abilities to make it come true. Accept that nothing will derail you, no matter how others may try to talk you down and away from it. How you show up helps or harms it. If you apologize for it or ignore it, your dream will slip away from you. If you treat it with respect, it will hang around because you've given it its due.

Connecting to and understanding your dream is one thing, but you must also commit to making it happen. It's a day-and-night responsibility. Belief and action—the two go hand in hand. Train, study, practice, produce, and grow with and into your dream and its full potential. That's what will make it come true and give you purpose.

Those truly living their best lives would not betray their dreams or themselves. They knew themselves and knew what they wanted. They didn't waste their dream time. They asked for what they wanted. They put their heart on the line. They saw and created opportunities. They hooked onto their dream and made it real, and they're happy.

When you commit to making your dreams come true, your whole heart and soul must be in them. You must know yourself and what you want; you must look for and create opportunities. You must agree to do whatever it takes to succeed (while remaining true to your values) and honor your dream life the way it deserves.

The Backup Plan

"You've gotta have a backup plan, something to fall back on," some may argue—particularly if you're in a creative field, where they expect you to fail and starve. I do not agree. As a matter of fact, I rather despise the idea and any talk of it because it creates fear that you won't make it.

The idea that you can't do it is insulting; that you should be ready to do something less important is destructive. *Aaaaah!* (That's me screaming.)

The "backup" idea is a cop-out. It weakens commitment, erodes confidence, and brings resistance right in on a golden barge.

Your inside heckler grabs all the attention, *So... not sure you can do this? Feeling inadequate? You should. Get out now! You'll get over it. The runner-up is not so bad.*

Having a "Plan B" removes the pressure and commitment. It's the easy way out of your heartfelt aspirations. From there, you tumble right into silence and disappointment, quietly smothering your hopes and wishes while walking away from what you love. It interrupts your potential to become who you are and who you're meant to be.

Instead, counter your inner heckler by giving one hundred percent of yourself to your dream. Choose to keep going, to do the work, and shove resistance aside. It takes courage and conviction, but isn't that what it always takes to dream big and live, to accomplish great things and be happy?

You may need to get a job to make money, but your dream work is different. A job outside your dream work should always be a means to an end—it should be moving you closer to your heart's desire rather than serving as a replacement.

Never give up on your dreams, no matter how old you are. It's never too late to make your life count. You still have a destiny, a calling...

4

Find Your Passion

Life is short; break the rules, forgive quickly, kiss slowly, love truly,
laugh uncontrollably, and never regret anything that made you smile.
Twenty years from now, you will be more disappointed by the things
you didn't do than by the ones you did. So, throw off the bowlines.
Sail away from the safe harbor. Catch the trade winds in your sails.
Explore. Dream. Discover.

—Mark Twain

How would you respond to the question, "What is your passion?" What lights you up? The answer is essential because that passion fuels the work.

Perhaps you're passionate about several things: golf, gardening, and painting, for example. It's great to have options. But oftentimes, there is one thing for which your heart truly yearns. It's the essence of who you are.

Your passion propels you to practice. It's what produces joy and the willingness to work at something. Let's say you have an unending desire to write. So, you commit to writing something every day, even when you don't have the words. You may find the simple act of writing produces a certain magic—with ideas and words seeming to flow on their own. Or you may find the day's work little more than gibberish; it doesn't stop you.

That commitment to your passion blends with and enhances all your dreams. If your passion is writing, maybe your work's been published a time or two; maybe your job relies on your writing skills—or perhaps you find ways to use them wherever you go, whatever you do . . . and that opens doors.

So yes, find your passion—find the desire to improve something in yourself, others, and possibly the world.

Passions Can Sneak Up on You

We each have gifts, some of which lie dormant inside us that we have yet to discover.

Growing up next door to our church, I considered becoming an altar boy or joining the choir. After attempting Latin, I figured choir was the easier choice. So, my mother spoke to Mary Ward, the organist, and, like that, I was in the choir. Ten years old and the only boy among fifteen girls, I loved to sing, learn harmonies, and be part of Mass and its ritual. I had nothing but respect for sacred music.

And then... I was asked to sing a solo.

The irony of singing "Oh Lord, I Am Not Worthy" when I most definitely did not feel worthy was not lost on me. But when I opened my mouth, the sound soared, echoing throughout the church. It held a gentle power; it encouraged me to express myself through words, rhythms, and various musical notes—high and low, major and minor. And just like that, I found my passion.

Mary said the angels gave me a voice. It was a gift from God. You have a gift as well.

If you haven't found it yet, don't worry. It's never too late to discover something new about yourself. Be open. Give things a try (even if you're scared of failing). You'll know it when you find it. It will make you happy. It will make you feel true to yourself. And the fact that it snuck up on you may make you love it even more.

Let Passion Drive You

Do you have a gut instinct to dig in and discover your passion—to see what it is and how it might be used to drive meaning and potential in your life? I hope you do.

You either sit with your passion and do very little with it (which is a crying shame and a waste), or you make up your mind to do the work to develop it: practice, improve, study, hone your craft, and make it something that matters . . . something that brings about positive change, well-being, and happiness. Passion can drive you to act and achieve your dreams, but you must choose to allow it to do so. This is all the more important when you are in your fifties, sixties, seventies, or older—when society expects you to put such things away.

No matter your age, passion sets you apart. You've just got to work at it, get good at it, and share it. Shakespeare did it. Hemingway, Maya Angelou, Walter Cronkite, Oprah, Seth Godin, Van Gogh, Georgia O'Keeffe, Augusta Savage, Joan Sutherland, Tony Bennett, and Beyoncé did it as well.

These people weren't born with success and a body of work. They were simply wise enough to let their passion drive their decisions and actions. You can do it too.

It Can Also Be a Choice

Now, if you're thinking, *What if I don't feel passionate about anything? What if passion is not a gift given to me by the gods? What if passion is overrated?* (Hint: you'll find some great resources to help you connect with your passion at michaelfeeleylifecoach.com/bonus)

Maybe think of it this way—a choice you can make to improve the outcome. Rather than focusing on an intense desire, consider it an attitude born of facts and logic that connect you to feelings that will prompt you to do things in life.

Passion doesn't have to be fireworks and bravura. It can be quiet and intensely focused. Introverts have passions, even if they're not standing on stages crowing about them. They may well choose to be in the background making scientific magic, which lights their internal flame.

In other words, don't let the demand to live and work by passion put too much pressure on you. It shouldn't limit and discourage you or create fear and self-doubt. That's just food for resistance. Why feed your inner bully who's just waiting to tell you that you don't have passion; you're a weirdo, a cold misfit?

You can activate passion in your life because you have something to share. For example, think of things you are proud of—projects you worked on or things you did that improved the lives of others. Let's call it your passionate worth. It has value because (most likely) you didn't coast along doing adequate work with those things. You rose to the challenge.

Passion seems effortless and empowering because you are doing what you love, and it gives you meaning. Passion can stir up compelling emotions or take a more structured, logical, measured, and realistic approach.

I encourage you to try. Commit to doing something. Work at contributing something that expresses you and see if and how passion appears. I'm confident it will.

Exercise: Connect With Your Passions

Take out a sheet of paper and answer these questions:

1. What do you have going on inside that would express you if it came out?

2. What do you want, hope, and need to develop?

3. How do you define passion?

4. What passions and dreams do you owe yourself and owe to others?

5. What are you passionately working on now?

Finally, I encourage you to always be yourself. Be true to who you are with all your passionate creativity and integrity. That's what you do better than anyone else on the face of the earth—being you.

5

Uncover Your Limiting Beliefs

"The illiterate of the 21st century will not be those who cannot read and write, but those who cannot learn, unlearn, and relearn."

—Alvin Toffler

Living life on your own terms, working somewhere that supports your values and appreciates your skills, and that also allows you to indulge your passions and satisfy your dreams . . . Isn't that what we all want? Then why is this so much harder than it sounds?

You've probably heard the term "limiting beliefs" before. Much as it sounds, they are simply beliefs that limit you in some way. When you accept a notion about the world, other people, or yourself (even if it's not true), it holds you captive.

Examples include:

You can't change after the age of twenty-five.

You must have a college degree to get ahead and be successful.

Women are not equal to men.

The good news is that you can change your limiting beliefs. It's important if you want to be happy and comfortable, remove stress from your life, and have solid, steady peace and harmony— if you want to live a life on your terms.

We each have limits. They might be physical, emotional, or ethical. If I'm a giant human being, I am not designed to be a jockey. To believe I am would set me up for frustration and failure. But we also make choices based on our beliefs that limit us.

You may not even know you have them. But if you feel stuck and indecisive, I can guarantee you do . . .

Maybe you believe you must retire at sixty-five because the system tells you it's time to quit and move on. You're too old to keep going, and you have had your time, so you should take your skills and knowledge and fade away.

Maybe you believe you have little to offer anymore. That there's no place for you.

What if, instead, you believe that you can create an opportunity at sixty-five to open a new business, something you have always wanted to do? What if you refuse to be limited by a number?

You make choices all day long about what's best for you. In some ways, these become your life values and how you view the world. Some of these choices may not serve you, but optimal or not, they all add up and make you who you are.

But you have freedom—the freedom of choice. You can decide to limit yourself, follow the retirement herd, keep your old head down, and refrain from asking questions. Or you can use your free will to stand for and move toward who you are and what you want.

You are not stuck or too old. That's the first thing you have to wrap your head around. Once you do that, you can see other limiting beliefs holding you back.

Un-limit Yourself

You can decide to un-limit yourself, to stop accepting that you're fated to be stuck, tied down, bored, unfulfilled, stationary, wasting away, and living the same old, same old.

By taking decisive action and crafting a strategic plan, you can break free from these self-imposed limits and open the door to new possibilities in your life and work. This shift will liberate you from feeling trapped and ignite a sense of dynamism and freedom, replacing stagnation with a renewed sense of purpose.

Your future will expand . . .

Unlimited—absolute—boundless—endless—immeasurable—immense—incalculable—indefinite—infinite—limitless—unconditional—unfettered—universal—unrestrained—unrestricted—untold—vast.

It's a call to action, the decision to live life without limits or restrictions. And it's powerful, inspiring, and liberating. It does more than simply prepare you for what you'll become in your next career; it's a whole approach to life.

For example:

Being a sculptor doesn't mean you can't draw with a pencil or paint with oils.

It doesn't mean you can't sing if you can't read music.

It doesn't mean you can't live in France if you don't speak French.

Writing with your right hand doesn't mean you can't learn to write with your left hand.

If you don't cook, it doesn't mean you can't attend the Auguste Escoffier School of Culinary Arts and learn.

The choice to do or not to do is right there. You can become and achieve whatever you want at any time in your entire life, legitimate limitations aside. (You don't need to tell me you'll never run a four-minute mile with a broken leg.) You have unlimited potential, which is the flip side of limiting beliefs.

How to Change Limiting Beliefs

Shaking your head, you may be thinking, *he clearly doesn't understand me or my situation.*

While that may be true to an extent, I know a thing or two about life and its ability to limit your beliefs about what's possible.

It's natural to build walls around yourself due to the opinions, choices, decisions, judgments, rules, expectations, and disappointments of those around you. It's easy to blame others for your unhappiness or troubles. You think you're protecting yourself. In reality, you may be doing more harm than good.

Instead, you need to critically examine yourself and your choices. Maybe you already know this but don't know how to do it—maybe the mere thought strikes fear in your heart.

It starts with a closer look at what you believe about your family, education, money, work, success, love, and happiness. Note the beliefs that block happiness, beliefs that prevent you from living a life of freedom and ease:

The world owes me something.

Life is a painful struggle and always will be—I was dealt a bad hand.

I've had to work hard for everything I ever had. Nothing was ever free or handed to me.

If good things happened, the rug would be pulled out from under me—that's what always happens.

I don't trust anyone.

Now, disprove those limiting beliefs by asking questions (teachers, consultants, and coaches can help).

Which leads us to this next exercise:

Exercise: Examine the Veracity of Your Belief

1. How true is that belief?

2. How does that belief limit you?

3. What evidence do you have to support that belief?

4. Where did you get that idea?

5. How well is that belief working for you?

6. How can you change that belief and let it go?

Once you see how a belief is limiting you, you can begin to refute and change it.

Let's take the belief that you're too old to be useful and valued . . .

Kenneth M. Dychwald, an American entrepreneur, gerontologist, and psychologist, wrote an article titled *The New Age of Aging*. In it, he suggests eighty is the new sixty. I believe it. You learn about age by living, not by boundaries. Imagination—desires—goals—plans—yearnings—passions—have no boundaries of age.

This calls to mind the story from a talented wise sage whom I love: "Some guy said to me, 'Don't you think you're too old to sing Rock 'n' Roll?' I said: 'You'd better check with Mick Jagger.'" The talented sage? Cher.

You change your limiting beliefs by thinking in new, positive ways. If you can't seem to get it done on your own, a good coach can help. They can show you how to turn on the light and see where you're going; stop pushing the car uphill, get inside, and step on the gas; create a map and enter unknown territory. And they'll offer insight throughout the process. Because it often takes an outsider to see what you can't see, too caught up in your current belief system.

Unlearning

For most of our lives, we fall into mindsets picked up from our families, schooling, work, economic strata, political affiliation, technology, friends, and society. These mindsets are not always beneficial. To remedy the situation, we need to unlearn or let go of some of these old (and unexamined) ways and practice new ones. How do we do that?

It begins with recognition. You must first understand that something you learned no longer works for you. It's led to an unjust, unfair, and untrue belief. Unlearning that belief can be deep, uncomfortable, and demanding. It may involve correcting false information and unlearning biases, prejudice, labeling, assumptions, and interpretations that harm you and other people, cultures, and ideas.

Despite the difficulty, it's a highly rewarding process because you're working to change the way you view the world. You're reconsidering things, changing your heart and mind. For example, let's say you've been led to believe a certain number indicates old age, feebleness, and irrelevance. Well, if you don't want to be perceived as old, feel old, think old, begin by being aware of the changes around you, and adopt new ways of thinking to keep up and flourish instead of being left behind.

Anything learned can be unlearned. Be patient. Be kind to yourself. It's never easy to break old patterns and build new opportunities. It takes commitment and deliberate practice. And don't be afraid to ask for help.

You relearn to learn again because there is a better way.

Potential

Speaking of beliefs that no longer serve, *harnessing your potential is something you do when you're twenty, not when you're old enough to remember Nixon.* To counter this belief, consider the definition of potential: "having or showing the capacity to become or develop into something in the future; existing in possibility."

Listen to what you tell yourself:

- I have the potential to be . . .
- I love doing . . .
- I always dream of being . . .
- I'm passionate about . . .
- No matter what, I'm going to . . .
- I'm really good at . . .
- My heart aches for . . .

Your capacity to achieve and be something is central to your potential; it's nearly always positive unless you have a propensity for laziness, negativity, complaining, and self-bloating (where we puff ourselves up and bloat our egos).

Question everything. The answers will get you unstuck and enable you to change and take steps toward growth and happiness. Why believe anything that limits you?

6

Learn to Trust the World

"Life loves to be taken by the lapel and told − 'I'm with you, kid. Let's go.'"
—Maya Angelou

Let's talk about trusting the world. It's the choice to see the world as for you, not against you. Trusting the world means focusing on optimistic emotions and believing that the world is on your side; it's not looking to harm or thwart you; instead, it is planning and supporting your happiness and success.

Granted, it can be challenging to trust the world when the news screams of rising prices and higher interest rates, cultural crises, political wrangling, and the latest war. Not to mention power-hungry billionaires, the climate change crisis, exploitation—the list goes on and on.

You've no doubt heard it said (maybe you've even been the one to say it), "The world needs to change." I see it differently. The world is fine the way it is. How you view it, on the other hand, could probably stand some adjustment.

Trust is one of our greatest virtues. It's part of human nature and one of our mightiest centering values. It's believing that someone or something (the world) is reliable and that good things will happen. There's security and confidence in trust.

Suppose you're contemplating a change in employment, worried you're about to be spat out of a company or into the great unknown. In that case, my take on trust may sound naïve. Trust and fear do not generally go hand in hand.

It's understandable. We're born with bundles of trust, but we learn through experience that we are either smart or foolish to trust situations, ourselves, and others. We may even question honesty and goodness, even the value of trust, since others have let us down.

For me, growing up was painful: an alcoholic father, parents with a grossly unhappy marriage, serious childhood illness, a lack of money, a society that didn't accept that I was gay, bullying. I saw the world as a hateful, messy place. However, through study and personal growth, I learned to see that my attitude toward the world was doing me no favors. I learned that this outlook was generally inaccurate, an untrue way of seeing those in authority, women, men, money, opportunity, sex, family, success, religion, freedom, and so on. I learned that I wasn't stuck with this point of view; I could change how I saw the world. When I did, I felt happier and so much more in control.

Let's be real. The world has dualities: good and evil, happiness and misery, love and hate, respect and contempt. Those identical opposites are in us all. We can be generous, selfish, kind, ruthless, helpful, and harmful. You can learn to trust yourself and trust the world despite these dualities. You can practice trust until you do. Will you make mistakes? Sure. But keep choosing to trust. The alternative will only make you feel worse and will yield bad results.

How to Build Trust

You first build trust in the world by becoming more trustworthy yourself. Trust is something to develop and maintain, not take for granted or play around with. Once trust is broken, it takes work to regain it. Broken trust destroys the confidence someone has in you, be it personal or professional.

When you trust someone, you count on their honesty. So be honest with yourself, and the rest will follow. Tell the truth. Be ethical. Keep your promises. The truth matters, and your self-respect and good name are on the line. Everything worth having is built on truth and trust—trust and truth.

You are continually building trust in whatever you do and wherever you go. If you work for the armed forces, you must trust yourself and those around you to survive. You cannot separate the two components. The same is true for a doctor, a lawyer, a teacher, a clergyperson, a contractor, an electrician, a housekeeper, a neighbor, a partner, a family member, and you. No matter your job, be trustworthy.

Even in great physical and emotional pain, you can still choose to believe the forces of the world will help you meet the challenge, and they usually do. Think of what you have already come through. Trust your ability to handle what comes your way. You've learned valuable lessons with each seemingly insurmountable challenge. Continue to trust and see the problems as opportunities to learn and grow.

Exercise: Trust Building

Answer the following questions in great detail:

1. How will you build trust in yourself and your work?

2. When has the truth ever let you down?

3. When was the last time you trusted the world, and it came through for you?

7

Gratitude for the Win

"Thank you" is the best prayer anyone could say. Thank you expresses extreme gratitude, humility, and understanding.

— Alice Walker

As you contemplate your career path, whether to stay in your current job or venture into a new vocation, be consciously grateful for all that exists around you and all that you experience. It can lead you toward success and self-empowerment, boost your productivity, help you avoid burnout, and steer you away from the narrow, weakening emotions that hold you back.

In his essay, *The Power of Gratitude*, Manfred Kets de Vries, professor of leadership and change at INSEAD, writes, "The words grateful and gratitude derive from the archaic adjective 'grate,' meaning pleasing to the mind, being full of gratitude, or being disposed to repay favors bestowed."

'Grate' originates from the Latin *gratis*, meaning the readiness to show appreciation for and to return kindness. Grateful people count their blessings, have the ability to appreciate the simple pleasures of life, and are always prepared to acknowledge whenever good things happen to them. They are also the kinds of people willing to give something back."

Gratitude changes your perspective on life. It allows you to express thanks, appreciation, pleasure, and positivity, which contributes to happiness. Conversely, ingratitude stirs up anger, resentment, irritation, negativity, and a sense of defeat and rejection. Ingratitude badly affects your mind and body, especially your heart. It drags you down, annihilating your deepest hope for happiness.

I'm not suggesting you ignore sadness or pain; simply allow gratitude to coexist. It motivates and moves you from victim mode into a higher place of positive energy. When you appreciate things, you're kinder, more hopeful, and stronger. And once you start to offer gratitude for things, you will surely find such things multiplying. It's life-giving. (And so important; that's why you'll find a resource to further develop gratitude at michaelfeeleylifecoach.com/bonus.)

Why You Need to Embrace Gratitude

When knee-deep in a job search process, it's easy to swing straight into anger and frustration when you run into one roadblock after another. You'll need gratitude to keep you afloat.

Be grateful that you can look for work, that you have a resume you're proud to send, that you can meet with people to introduce your abilities, and that you can learn and grow from each conversation. It's the height of professionalism.

That's why the most successful companies have a thriving culture of gratitude, and they work to maintain it. You'll want to get a feel for this quality as you interview. Operating in such an environment makes you far more likely to enjoy those around you because gratitude builds emotional intelligence (EI) and empathy. It's directly related to compassion and forgiveness, which are critical in the daily work environment.

Gratitude has a simple, lasting ability to give strength and clarity in a moment. Thinking and expressing what you're grateful for is a potent antidote to negativity, stress, and despair. It also fosters respect for others, which allows you to hold on even when you think you can't last another minute. I've seen it in the lives of my clients and in my own life as well.

I once worked with a man we'll call Bill. Bill would go behind my back and do anything to make money. He betrayed my trust and harmed my work and reputation with clients. To say I disliked and distrusted him would be an understatement. Before long, anger consumed me to the point of being unhealthy. I loved my work, and he wasn't going anywhere. Something had to change.

So, I gave myself an assignment: *each day, I wrote one sentence about what I respected about Bill.* The choice to respect certainly goes against the grain; it wasn't a standard choice for a fellow worker who seemed to be unethical. But my purpose was to change my disdain for him because it was hurtful to me.

I will not lie; it was incredibly hard to get past my rage and find one simple, genuine example of respect for him.

Here are some examples:

I respect Bill for being on time to work every day.

I respect the fact that he dresses professionally.

I respect Bill for having a high school degree and a college degree in English.

Bill is a single parent, and I respect him for supporting his two children financially.

Education is important to Bill, and I respect him for sending his children to good schools.

I respect Bill for writing short stories and having some of them published.

They were all facts that merited respect and gratitude.

The more I learned about Bill, with a focus on respect, the less angry I became. In its place was empathy and wonder. I had misjudged him in many ways. While I didn't want or need to become his friend, my study of Bill changed my rage to greater peace of mind and even compassion. I just needed to find a way to better myself and my work environment.

If you find yourself in a similar situation, give it a try. Showing respect promotes gratitude and care for others. It also keeps you from acting precipitously. Not to mention, goodwill is tough and mighty stuff. Chances are good; if you send it out, it will come back to you.

Cultivating Gratitude

Cultivating gratitude is an intelligent and easy way to enrich your life. And by cultivating, I mean practice. Practice gratitude, and soon enough, it will become a natural, organic way to live. It increases the good when you like things and appreciate what's good. It builds self-esteem, hope, and joy. When you're thankful, you're more confident and happier. Gratitude always increases you, not depletes you. You're more yourself, not less. It's a daily part of a healthy lifestyle.

Think of it as a mammoth savings account where you deposit good feelings, positive emotions, and thankfulness. It's your personal reserve for strength and happiness — open for business twenty-four hours a day, seven days a week, three hundred sixty-five days a year.

If you're stressed, tired, or overwhelmed with work or projects, tap into your gratitude account and write it down: "I'm grateful for stars at night ... grateful for good health ... grateful for having true love these past twenty-eight years ... for blue skies, fresh water, and healthy senses."

Chances are good that you'll immediately begin to feel peace and clarity.

Exercise: Add to Your Gratitude Account

There are many ways to fill up your gratitude account; here are three steps to get you started:

1. Call it "intentional gratitude" or "conscious appreciation," but build a new habit of expressing specific gratitude frequently. It will make you feel fortunate and kind.

2. Create a specific daily mantra for yourself — a prayer, wish, vow, or commitment:

   "Gratitude makes me strong. Gratitude refreshes me. I am grateful for_____." Keep it in mind. Say it to people. Write it in notes and emails.

3. "Thank you" takes one second to say. Consciously look for opportunities to express gratitude and do good things often. Don't miss an opportunity to be thankful.

Exercise: Start a Daily Gratitude Journal.

Write three things you're grateful for every night before bed.

1. How does gratitude live in the world? Look for examples in music, art, literature, daily life, history, and people you see and know. Document the gratitude you find.

2. Acknowledge negativity and instantly counter it with genuine appreciation and thanks. See what happens to you. Test gratitude.

3. Think about someone you're grateful for. Take a few moments to see why you're thankful. What is the specific reason? What did you benefit from or receive from them that you're grateful for? Then go right ahead and thank them. Call, email, write a letter, or send a prayer expressing your gratitude. See what happens to you and to them when you say thank you.

Gratitude is a tool that you can count on and benefit from immediately. It's your true nature, your essence, your center, one of the deepest emotions you (okay, all people) have. And get this . . . you're born with an endless supply of gratitude you can tap into at any time.

Gratitude remains. It never lets you down.

Albert Einstein (someone famous for being logical and scientific) described it like this: "There are only two ways to live: you can live as if nothing is a miracle; you can live as if everything is a miracle." Why not choose to be grateful for the little miracles all around you?

There are loads of things to be grateful for in an instant. All you have to do is be conscious of them.

PART II:
CONQUERING
FEARS

8

The Fear of Rejection

An opportunity always looks like a lucky break.
It happens when you encounter the possibility of making a huge jump
toward the life your essential self wants to live.
—Dr. Martha Beck

At some point in your career, the fear of rejection will come knocking at the door. It'll knock so loudly that you'll only want to cling to what you know, even if you're unhappy. The key is to get to know that fear, to see it in a new light, and to act anyway.

Personally, I have a healthy relationship with rejection, which some people find curious.

Part of it stems from my childhood, where the feeling of rejection was immense from very early on. It was ingrained in everyday life. In response, I decided not to be a victim or a failure. I was going to live life on my terms, which served me well in my chosen profession as an actor.

One particular audition comes to mind. I had called my agent and asked him to submit me because I'd be perfect for the part. He told me that the powers that be weren't seeing non-union actors. "You don't stand a chance."

But I knew I stood a chance and was taking it. I knew I could sing the hell out of that song, and when they heard me, they'd give me the part of *The Corporal*. I'd been there since eight-thirty that morning. The director was eating in. I wasn't going to miss my chance.

There I was, Michael Feeley, sitting on one of those uncomfortable folding chairs, waiting it out. Because... I felt it in my gut. I knew it would happen!

The door opened at four-thirty in the afternoon, and the director came out. "Thanks, everyone, for coming in. The musical is cast."

I stood up. "Wait, please! You've got to hear me sing because you'll give me the part when you do." The room went still. I didn't care what they thought. I was asking for what I wanted. Rejection mattered not one whit.

"Alright," the director said. "Come on in and sing."

I sang "Danny Boy," the Irish air with the same feeling as the show's solo, "The Only Home I Know." It had the same lyric tenor quality, soaring high notes, and the emotional theme of war, love, and going home.

After I finished, the director studied me for a good long time; he looked at my resume and headshot. After quietly talking to the musical conductor and pianist back and forth for several minutes, he finally turned to me and said, "Hello, Corporal. The part is yours." I didn't have an Equity Card, but he would ensure I got one to work in a Broadway touring company. "People will love hearing you. Thank you for standing up and asking to sing."

Perhaps looking at rejection the same way will reduce your fears now that you're considering the next big chapter in your work life.

How to Look at Rejection

Maybe you didn't get the promotion; you've been cordially invited to find another job; you're smack dab in the middle of the interview process. Each can be seen as a rejection. *Rejected... not accepted... you don't like me... you don't want me... I'm not good enough,* that's how most see rejection. It's one of our greatest fears—the possibility of being rejected by others and ourselves. Rejecting yourself, I should add, is as simple as saying, "I hate myself and my life."

But the truth is, we all experience rejection and failure. While some take it personally and are daunted and frustrated by it, others are motivated by it. Even highly successful people fail and are rejected, but they learn from it because they have a career goal and purpose. They keep fine-tuning their work and strategically refining their plan. They're prepared to keep moving through the rejection and seldom take no for an answer.

In fact, in the face of rejection, they look for other ways to be approved because they are determined to succeed. They keep trying to get what they want because they have confidence in themselves and what they offer. They don't give up. They aren't pushy or obnoxious in their pursuit of getting ahead, but they do flip rejection into empowerment by going after more. They keep what works and improve what doesn't.

Rejections can limit or even ruin your life, but they are not the truth. Choose to look at rejection not as a source of pain but as a challenge to improve until you get what you want.

There's more than one way to get it done, so why sweat it?

Make Friends with Rejection

Rejection can be your friend. It's an opportunity to learn and change, improve your work, and grow. It starts with being curious: what was indeed rejected; were you refused, or was your project and presentation rejected? If your work was rejected, it doesn't necessarily mean you were rejected. Sometimes it's simply a matter of odds. Only one person was successful; the others were not.

Be aware of the risks, competition, and the unknown, but focus on what you can control—your credentials, skills, abilities, attitude, and values. Be yourself and give all you can. Don't hold back.

Will you be rejected? It's possible. Prepare for it. But take responsibility. Did you mess up? Could you have done more or been better? Where do you go from here? This is where your goals, plans, and strategies come in.

Exercise: Navigating a Failure

Ask yourself the following questions:

1. What is my next step if I fail to get what I want? What might plan B, C, or W be?

2. What have I learned from this loss?

3. How can I release a feeling of self-blame and doubt?

4. Where was I successful in the application, interview, and product release?

5. Where am I proud of myself for the choice and action steps I took to try?

6. How can I celebrate taking the risk?

7. Where could I have done better?

8. Even with a loss, where am I grateful?

9. Where can rejection be for the best?

10. Where am I still successful and worthy?

Counter the letdowns with a positive mindset. This will help you be logical and resilient. Allow your friendship with rejection to strengthen rather than weaken you. Then, continue to hope and prepare for more until you get what you want.

Know When to Quit

You failed to get the job. You failed in some way to please people and have them see how valuable you are, as well as your skills and work ethic. If you keep working at something and it's not happening, it's easy to feel like a total failure. So, see the truth—it may be time to stop and make an important change.

Before you do, evaluate rejection in the light of day. Consider yourself and your work. What works and what doesn't? Are you doing, creating, and pursuing something achievable, realistic, and practical? Is it something people are looking for?

Knowing your skills is the first part; you must go deeper and critically understand what differentiates you from the masses and your immediate competition. Think about it:

- What makes you rare?
- What makes your skills unique, desired, and sought after?
- What will people gain by hiring you?
- What will people stand to lose if they do not hire you?

You want to lead with scarcity. By that, I mean knowing what's missing in an open job, marketplace, service, and products. Then, you can point it out and explain how you can fill it.

Loss can help motivate people to act positively in your favor.

Rejection can make you stronger. It can help you recognize when you need to quit. And by quitting, I don't mean giving up on your dreams. It's letting go of the stubborn refusal to achieve them in a different way. After all, some plants survive droughts, and some do not. Some may not do well in a specific location, but when transplanted, they thrive.

Above all, remember that rejection doesn't lessen your value. It doesn't lower the importance of who you are, your skills, abilities, life experiences, or, most importantly, the meaning of your life. Your life matters.

9

The Fear of Competition

Competition ignites passion, determination, and the pursuit of excellence.
—**Serena Williams**

You will face competition if you plan to stay in your current job, transition to a similar role in a different company, or shift to a new career path. It's part of life. The fear of competition can affect you negatively; it can cause stress, self-doubt, decreased motivation, or even poor performance. The key is not to let this fear run the show. You want to learn how to harness competition in your favor. And it all comes back to knowing yourself and what you bring to the table.

Knowing your skills, relevant experience, and unique contributions is one of the best ways to dampen the fear of being found wanting when you are about to be compared to others. That means identifying your credentials, listing your successful work projects, and being able to recite your history, experience, connections, and assets the way you would your phone number.

Consider Olympic athletes. They constantly compete against the best of the best in their fields. They use that competition to fuel their commitment, training schedule, and desire to be at the top. So, when it comes time to go head-to-head with the competition, they do so with professionalism and confidence. You need to do the same. Meet your competition with this mindset: *Bring it on. I'm eager. I'm ready.*

Competence Beats Competition

You know others are vying for your position or the opportunities you want. That means you must prepare to present, promote, and sell yourself, complete with your unique value proposition. You need to make it clear that you are the logical choice for the position—you and you alone, regardless of the other candidates waiting in the wings.

Listen up if you're afraid of what's lurking in the wings.

Confidence in training and experience will help you thrive in the face of competition. Know what you're good at and that you have a lot to give. It's not arrogance; it's a focus on the work and producing your best material. When you do, you will seldom, if ever, think about the competition. It simply comes down to logic. You will get the job, or you won't; either way, you'll be damn sure you gave it one hell of a try in all ways.

Focus on competence rather than the competition. Hone your skills. Be creative and spontaneous. Find unique ways that you can meet their needs. In doing so, you'll help others choose you. Then, when opportunity knocks, you can open the door, show it your best hospitality and innovation, and make things happen.

A Fresh Way to Look at Competition

Our fear of competition tends to be rooted in a fear that we won't measure up—that someone will take something that we desire. However, the origin of the word competition is not "against" but "to strive together." Sure, you want to win. We all do. But the emphasis is no longer the need to win at all costs. It's no longer combative in nature. You're all in it together.

This change in viewpoint can have a positive effect in a couple of different ways. Rather than being a big, bad Boogey Man, the person competing against you is simply a possibility, much like you. This should inspire you to be the best you can be.

Second, viewing the competition as fellow human beings offers a certain freedom to be bold yet respectful in asking for what you want—to help others see your value.

Some survivors choose to live out their careers in suboptimal work environments because they're too afraid to reach for what they really want. They feel as though they can't compete, so they often take a morally superior stance. *People who can compete are selfish cut-throats who don't care who they step on.* Such thoughts give them an out because they don't have to try. They don't have to risk feeling like a loser. They get to be a good person instead of a successful person. It's like this weird loophole they create for themselves, which only leaves them unhappy and playing small, playing the victim.

You can see yourself against all of them, or you can see yourself making a great effort together.

I Get Survival Mode

I grew up in a home where I competed to survive. That's how I got through my parents' painful marriage, my dad's drinking, a deadly childhood illness, being gay, and incessant bullying.

Through observation, I learned to fight for myself, be harsh and cruel, hate, and hurl vulgar insults. I could verbally cut someone down (I'm not talking about Oscar Wilde-style satire). No, I was vindictive. I lashed out to destroy, cutting right into the weaknesses of others, especially those of my dad, letting him know what a drunken failure he was.

You can't live in such an environment and not participate, fight for your life, or be damaged goods, no matter how much you hide, pretend, and keep silent.

But in every circumstance, you have a choice of how you'll respond.

I pushed forward and decided never to live that way again. I was a survivor of adversity by choice, not accident or luck. I could have stayed a victim, held back, and told myself I didn't deserve good things. Instead, I chose to live life on my terms. And then, I made it happen through hard work and dedication.

It may sound corny, but it's true: you don't have to come from a rose garden to be a rose.

You will discover that for yourself. You're uncovering your worth. Be open, giving, kind, generous, strong, and grateful. Don't be afraid to say, "This is who I am." Take it on. Say it out loud. Own it.

You're a survivor, too—a resilient, resourceful, determined spirit. If the word survivor doesn't work for you, consider one of these: succeeder, accomplisher, achiever, winner.

Maybe you're curious about things; you're a wonderer. Curiosity is often directly connected to solving a problem and getting positive results. You've most likely come through things and created ways to cope with difficulties and successes personally and professionally.

I'm confident you're up to the career changes you are strategizing.

You've nothing to fear from the competition. They're all part of figuring out who you are and what you want, and they just might help you get it.

10

The Fear of Bullying

Resistance's goal is not to wound or disable. Resistance aims to kill.
Its target is the epicenter of our being: our genius, our soul,
the unique and priceless gift we were put on this earth to give and
that no one else has but us. Resistance means business.
When we fight it, we are in a war to the death.

—Steven Pressfield

You're at a crossroads with your career. You may be miserable in your current position yet terrified to move on. *What if I jump from the frying pan straight into the fire?* You may feel underappreciated, even bullied. Some jerk is ensuring you never get that promotion or raise out of pure spite. You fear you're a magnet for such abuse. Better the devil you know than the devil you don't. You'd rather quit or retire, even though you don't have the financial resources to entertain the option. If any of these ring true, we need to discuss workplace bullying and resistance, code for inner bullying.

Brainstorm "bully," and the following may come to mind:

Consistent harm on purpose

Intimidation

Torment

Aggressive dominance

Tyrannizing

Oppression

Persecution

Browbeating

Insult-slinging

Doesn't sound too appealing; it's not exactly something you'd like to participate in or receive. Yet bullying happens everywhere: in families, the schoolyard, on social media, and at work. It crops up in all professions.

It tends to key in on age, disability, nationality, race, religion, gender, or sexual orientation.

Noncombative personality types, deep introverts, or those with a quirky way of looking at the world are easy targets. Whatever the catalyst, bullying is all about unacceptable physical and mental abuse and the need for the bully to have power.

The only way to change the abuse is to stand up to it, to oppose it, to actively do whatever it takes to end the brutality. But first, you have to lose the fear of it. If you don't, you'll be unhappy wherever you are.

I Know Bullies

Easy for you to say, you may be thinking. *You're not living in hell for the sake of a paycheck.*

But I do know bullying...

I was bullied throughout junior high and high school. Even though I had good grades and was respected for my skills in acting and music—even though I did my best to cover up my differences—some people saw that I was not like them and viciously went after me. Fem, faggot, queer, homo... I heard them all. Many of my classmates physically threatened me.

Have you ever been hated? Have you felt the cruelty of bigotry? It makes your life a living hell every single day.

Maybe you know.

Get bullied like that, and you don't want to go out. You live in fear. You might not worry about group mobbing and physical threats in the coffee room, but you know what it's like to live with rumors, maybe even groping or entrapment. Your stomach twists into a horrible knot when someone you must work with, or who stands between you and career success, walks in and spots you. You hope and pray that you don't see those ruining your life—yet there they are. You want to die, at times, or you wish it on them so you can be happy again without constant fear and pain.

These are the same feelings I felt as a gay kid in the 1960s.

Back then, I shied away from standing up to my bullies because I was terrified of being physically hurt, broken, and scarred. I believed that if I fought back, I'd be fighting forever. Like being the fastest draw in the West, where everyone comes gunning for you to make a name for themselves.

I never bothered to tell my parents about the daily pain I endured because they would have only made it worse. My friends and teachers knew of my ordeal, but few came forward to stop it or help me understand and better live with it. They kept silent, which is one of the most shameful and cowardly decisions people make because it promotes cruelty in our society.

Sometimes, the others standing by as you take an insult or get relegated to an office the size of a supply closet makes you feel the worst. As a young person, you hope someone will step in to fight for you and save you. As an adult, you have the choice to do something about it; this may include meeting with Human Resources or your manager to address the ill will.

The bottom line: you do not have to be afraid of bullies; you do not have to tolerate bullying at work or in any other place in your life. Recruit other people. Call them in to confront and change what is happening and put an end to the inhumane activity. And if you have the chance, stand up for fairness and justice for others.

A Caveat

There are risks and rewards when confronting a bully, one-on-one or with others present. There is the added fear that confrontation with a bully at work could further disrupt your job, including the possibility of losing your job if the bullying comes from your boss or other higher-up officials. You may also harm your reputation in and outside of work, earning the name of a troublemaker who is challenging to work with.

After publishing an article on bullying, a colleague wrote to me and shared an incident he had experienced at work. I was horrified, deeply saddened, and moved by his courage to talk about what he endured—how he suffered mentally and physically and was driven to create a change for his welfare. If you knew this man, you would never have imagined that anyone would bully him because of his physical stature, kindness, work ethic, skills, creativity, and the respect he received from fellow workers. The bully undoubtedly hated these attributes and went in to destroy them.

"I once had to deal with a bully in my workplace... I tolerated the situation for three years because I felt the need to continue doing my job. When it became clear that the bully's behavior wouldn't change, even after I addressed it directly with the bully and others on the team, I knew I had to transfer out despite enjoying my work.

"In some companies, going to HR can have negative consequences, as it can label you as a troublemaker regardless of your work ethic or character, and other departments may not want to work with you. Additionally, I had to keep my transfer plans secret, as any disciplinary action could prevent me from transferring, and I knew the bully might try to use that against me.

"Luckily, a position opened up in another division of the firm, and I was able to interview without the bully knowing.

"They asked me why I wanted to leave and what it would take to get me to stay, but I didn't want to cause any trouble, so I simply told them I wanted to 'learn more about the company.'

"With the bully, I was under so much stress and anxiety that the rest of my life and interests suffered. I even got shingles at one point. After I left, the team fell apart because I might have been their mule and linchpin, and the bully soon after was out of a job.

"I am doing much better 'learning more about the company,' and the new people I am with have been great. They have positive goals and expectations that help us to perform and train people far better than other teams. I am grateful each day I show up at work. Even though it has been six years, I feel relieved that I am not being bullied anymore. I remember not to do it to others. When my team leader starts down that path, I can point out unhealthy behaviors to correct things early."

It's important to recognize the risks and rewards of confronting a bully. Thankfully, as this example illustrates, the rewards often outweigh the risks.

Recovering From Bullying

When you're bullied, you may blame yourself for being attacked. What's wrong with me? What did I do to attract this kind of hatred in my life? What did I do to the people who go after me?

You start acting differently. You pretend to be something and someone else: you hide behind a look of indifference; you appear untouchable. Before long, your talents, skills, values, and dreams are long forgotten. You stop looking for help, for answers, for understanding.

To be the hero of the story, not only do you have to stand up to bullies, but you must also learn to recover from their abuse. Only then can you break their dominance over you once and for all.

Two steps help in the recovery process:

Step 1: Start With Empathy

As crazy as it sounds, you need to have empathy for bullies. Have empathy for someone who torments me? Is this a joke? No. I'm deeply serious. When you begin to understand the reasons people bully, it will help you recover your power and dignity.

People bully others for many reasons (none of them good). Perhaps they have been abused in some way and use their hurt to hurt others. Perhaps bullying is stress-related. The bully has experienced trauma, their home life is impossible, or their marriage is on the fritz. People act in all sorts of ways to protect themselves.

I can all but guarantee that the bully feels bad about themselves (even if they may not admit it). Bullying may be a learned behavior. They've been told that to be a man, you can't show emotions because it's weak or even effeminate. Perhaps they're insecure about their friends and lifestyle; maybe they're trying to become immune to being bullied themselves.

Whatever the reason, they've made choices to protect themselves with some control; bitching, talking against people, and threatening others are protective and unfortunate behaviors they rely on to get through life.

Learn as much as possible about your bully and why bullies are the way they are.

Knowledge is freedom and strength. And it gives you the courage to forgive. You don't have to forget, but in releasing your hatred, you can be free of their control over you.

Step 2: Tell a Better Story

How you view the traumatic experience of being bullied doesn't have to be debilitating; it can be life-enhancing. You can reframe and create new interpretations that allow you to clear and heal old wounds that lock you down.

You have two stories to tell about everything in your life. Both are true, but the difference lies in your purpose and its effect on you and others.

One story...

I was a victim of bullying in school. It ruined my life every single day. I lived in constant fear. My stomach was tied up in knots. I despised the people who relentlessly tortured me. I had a right to hate the world and seek revenge. Why me? What did I do to these monsters?

Another possibility...

I was bullied in school, but I'm no one's victim. It was hell every single day, but the fear and hatred I felt taught me never to cause another person pain in any way. I found happiness and relief from bullying in music, acting, and art. That's where I liked the world most, where I forgot about my pain. Bullies are insecure people looking for power and control. I may never know what is going on in the life of a bully. Perhaps they were bullied at home. Thinking about that, having compassion releases my pain. I'm no longer under their control.

The same story, but two ways of seeing the world; two different mindsets.

We can see with gratitude or resentment. We can choose goodwill or retaliate, be compassionate to others and ourselves, or live with malice.

It sounds wild to say, but it's true: I'm grateful I was bullied. It enabled me to help others contend with their own bullies and made me a kinder person. Sometimes, to know kindness, we must experience unkindness.

Mind you, there's no excuse for cruelty of any kind. That's not what I'm saying. The point is that when you change how you think about bullying, it changes its effect on you. If you tell your story as a tragedy, chances are good it will be a tragedy. You cannot dwell in misery forever and expect to thrive. Adversity can be an advantage. Every tough story has a flip side that calls to our humanity and gives us peace of mind and heart.

The Inner Bully

If you've been bullied, I bet you've also got an inner bully. That little voice inside your head says you deserve bad treatment, that you'll never amount to anything, so why bother?

It starts with resistance.

Resistance is all about fear: fear of rejection, success, failure, change, trying (or not trying)—any fear that limits and stops you from being true to yourself. It makes you forget your worth, dreams, skills, and even your humanity.

Resistance is real. Perhaps you've heard of the amygdala, also known as the lizard brain, inner critic, dark shadow, narrow self, or gremlin. It's the part of the brain that processes emotions, most notably fear. Its job is to detect potential threats and trigger fight-or-flight responses. Hence, resistance is intended to keep you safe.

But it's a bit like auto-correct; it's not always helpful. To keep you safe, it cuts you down by keeping you small and controlled. It equates safety with familiarity, even if what's familiar isn't serving you.

Accepting the status quo can seem like an easy way out. You don't have to change (your inner bully may go as far as to say you can't); you don't have to do too much work to achieve what you hope for because it doesn't matter anyway.

Your inner bully is as real as any workplace bully that taunts you, pokes at you, knocks you down, and says, "Hey, crybaby. You'll never succeed. You don't have what it takes."

Awareness and understanding are the first steps to fighting back. Listen carefully; stand up for yourself and your dreams if your inner voice aims to undervalue, underestimate, and undermine you to keep you safe in the known. You have a passion. Your work is valuable—and it will improve the lives of others.

Bullies like having power, including the one living in your head. They try to stop you from being who you truly are and succeeding at what you hope to achieve through fear and self-doubt. It's your job to be fearless, to face your inner bully, and to take control of your life. Think of it this way: there is pleasure in being fearless; you get to fear less. (If you could use more help taming your inner bully, look to the resource section at michaelfeeleylifecoach.com/bonus)

Call Out Your Bully

Believe it or not, fear and doubt are crucial, red-flared positive signals. They guide you forward, show that your work matters, and allow you to succeed. Otherwise, they wouldn't be there. Trust that your inner bully is showing up for a good reason.

So, become something of a stalker. Study what brings your heckler out. When does it appear, and why?

When you know the specific reason for bully talk—be it stress, decision-making, learning something new, changing your life, or heading toward success—you'll be prepared. You can send that bully packing when he shows up. Push him around and chase him down the street for a change.

Exercise: Your Inner Bully Diary

Keep an Inner Bully Diary. List the facts. Collect and examine the evidence. Record it:

1.   When does it show up?

2.   What does it specifically say to you?

Example: It is not generic talk. My bully tells me, "You'll never be good enough. You'll always be second best. You're a shallow lightweight. When you talk, no one listens."

3.   What happens when you confront it, send it away, or sit with your heckler?

Fear is vital for growth and change. You will become a better person when you conquer it (and the associated anxiety). It will motivate you to meet new people, try new things, take risks, look for new opportunities, and explore the unknown.

It's your job, intense and demanding as it may be, to break through your fears, to change, and go after living your dreams. Never let anyone, least of all yourself, make less of who you are. Don't sell out your soul!

Give Your Bully a New Job

You need to challenge your inner bully and challenge yourself to be strong and confident. It allows you to move forward beyond the reach of doubt, anxiety, blame, and even self-pity. Since this step requires that you recognize your inner bully, why not give it form? Create an image, an actual doll or being, or an item representing your bully. This helps take away its power and make it real.

My inner bully is called Max. He's a piano player in a dark bar who welcomes you in, gets to know your story and all your weaknesses, and then uses them against you. One of his favorite songs to play for me is "Forgettable, That's What You Are". Another is, "You're Nobody, and You'll Always be Nobody to Me".

Obviously, a bully is good at "putting you in your place," of keeping you down: I can't do that... I'll never be able to... That's not me... Everyone else is so much more creative, popular, beautiful...

Hopefully, by now, you're recognizing limiting beliefs. They reveal low self-esteem, a lack of confidence in your abilities and knowledge, and worry about what others think about you. They also show you what you need to work on. They help you see the truth and clear the pathway for change.

So, why not assign your inner bully a new job? Give him a big promotion and ask for his help. A good critic of anything (theater, music, art, sports) is a teacher. They present what's good and what could be better. See your inner critic like that. Listen. If there's one percent truth in it, take it and learn.

Discovering the truth about yourself, even your shortcomings, faults, or weaknesses, is beautiful and necessary work. It allows you to live your life with greatness, honesty, and unconditional love. Calling out your inner bully means calling out the best things in yourself.

11

The Fear of
Not Being Good Enough

---

*"There is no passion to be found in playing small—in
settling for a life that is less than the one you are capable of living."*
– **Nelson Mandela**

Being human, you naturally fear not measuring up. *Not Good Enough*—the mere thought can paralyze you, make you feel worthless and empty, and cause you to question your abilities, knowledge, skills, personality, and character. But remember, you are not the only one with this fear. In fact, the extreme version of it has a name: atelophobia, where *everything* you do is judged through a personal lens of not being good enough, right down to how you tie your shoelaces. Under the influence of atelophobia, you can fiercely blame and punish yourself, easily undermine yourself, feel disappointed in yourself, and project it onto others. *If you see how lousy you are, surely they do, too!*

Now, bear with me while I tell you a story. You'll spot its relevance soon enough . . .

When email first arrived in our headhunting office and we were all required to use it, I panicked. Not only were my tech skills weak, but they were also non-existent. I went right down the hopeless tech tubes and believed I would need to quit my job; my career was over. I was completely vulnerable. *I'll never be good enough for this.*

An immensely kind lady I worked with saw my panic and fear and offered to help. She assured me it was easy and went to work setting up my email address and teaching me how to navigate the system. She stayed with me for days, with unlimited goodwill for me. I was no longer alone—she helped me see I could learn and change.

When you connect with others, vulnerability changes to hope. With a bit of work and a little support, "I can't" turns to "I can . . . I will succeed."

Combating the Fear

You could be the president of your local Rotary Club, play the trumpet in a jazz band, and be the fastest member of the vintage softball team—receiving all kinds of praise—but still think you're not so good; you don't deserve all the accolades; if people really knew you, they'd see what a fraud you are. The fear of not being good enough can happen to anyone at any age.

It's a form of resistance. And you combat it by sticking to the facts. Tell the truth about yourself instead of defaulting to a defeatist mindset. For instance, if you feel inadequate because you didn't get a promotion, remind yourself of your past successes and the positive feedback you've received. This can help you see the situation more objectively.

Now, here's the thing. Sometimes, your fear of not being good enough has a seed of truth in it. That's why sticking to the facts is important. They can help you determine if that's the case so you can right the ship and get the results you claim to want to enjoy. Sometimes, you are not good enough and must be honest with yourself.

For instance, let's say you're applying for a job that requires fluent Castilian Spanish—speaking, reading, and writing. You're a master at speaking the language; your reading skills are fifty-fifty, but your writing is not so good. You've got to look at the facts and determine if you're right for the job or setting yourself up for failure. If the sum of all parts equals no, you are not qualified in all ways. With kindness to yourself, it's fair to say, in this instance, that you may not be good enough.

The Truth Will Set You Free

Be grateful for the truth, get comfortable with it, and then move forward. Or you can beat yourself up and rave about the injustice of it all. It's your choice.

I'd suggest being inspired by the truth. It can encourage you to improve—to study, learn, and practice—so you can add more value. It's a bit like erasing the "not good enough" so you can get on with the task at hand.

What you're after, now more than ever, is factual awareness.

What is the truth about you? That's the question you must constantly answer, particularly when considering your next career move. Keep asking; keep digging in: where you are good, where you are enough . . . and where you are not.

The truth sets boundaries and creates freedom, opportunities, confidence, inspiration, power, happiness, gratitude, and success. Let the truth create trust in yourself and move you forward.

The Pluses and Minuses of Vulnerability

Fear makes us feel vulnerable, and vulnerability can seem like a weakness, a lack of self-confidence and control. You don't want to wear that kind of cologne when you're in the job market.

However, vulnerability can also be a powerful tool for change. Admitting a weakness, as opposed to overcompensating to avoid detection, can inspire true change. Vulnerability is a space where you can appreciate your talents and skills without hiding the facts. You can feel secure in your own skin. You can express what you feel to others, including your willingness to take risks and how good and capable you are.

Let's go back to the Castilian Spanish job opportunity I mentioned to expand on this idea further. You want to be honest.

Admit your lack of reading and writing skills . . . at the present. But offer to bring those up to speed within a six-month probation period to show how good and capable you are.

It's an empowering shift in mindset from inadequate to adequate—ample—acceptable—sufficient—relevant—a glorious work in progress, which is the opposite of lacking and feeling deficient, like a fake who is about to get caught in a web of lies.

At the heart of vulnerability is trust: in your capabilities and worth, in the world to support and empower you, and in others.

Here's an example from my own life . . .

Once upon a time, I auditioned for a role in *The Bus and Truck Tour* of *Jesus Christ Superstar*. (Props, costumes, and staging are in a truck, and the actors and musicians are in a bus. You drive from one booking to another. Set up, do the show, take it all down, get back in the bus and truck, drive to a new place, and do it again.) It might be worth doing for the right role, actors, and director, but the working conditions are not ideal.

The powers that be asked me to sing a song with many high notes, which I did. I finished, and the director said, "Sing it again."

I did.

"Sing it again."

So, I did.

"Sing it again."

I sang it five times in a row.

"Do you think you can do that every night?" the director asked.

"Are you kidding me? Absolutely! I'm trained. You heard it."

"I'm not sure you can."

I thanked him and started to walk off stage, confident this opportunity was not worth it. It seemed the director didn't know what he was doing. I wasn't shaken by his insinuation. Perhaps he wanted me to be unsure, to take a whack at my confidence. Who knows?

"Hey, we're not finished," he said.

"Yes. We are," I countered.

I had good technique and training, was unafraid to show my emotions, and had staying power. I seldom quit, but some people missed what was right in front of them, and that ringing alarm bell needed to be heeded.

Saying no to work you love can be tough, but it is also a way to maintain self-respect while being vulnerable.

You are always vulnerable when auditioning or interviewing because you hope to get the job, and you're never sure of what the casting people, director, or interviewer have in mind. You also need to trust yourself. Trust your skills and gut instinct; never let anyone manipulate you into doubting yourself. Recognize it right away and decide what you want to do.

Exercise: The Truth About What You're Good At

1. List three people, clients, friends, or partners who unequivocally see value in you.

2. What is the one thing you are proudest of in your life?

> 3. Name one problem you solved that helped another person or people live better.
> 4. What personal challenge have you lived through that strengthened you and why?

The answers are the life facts that oppose the "I'm not good enough" force. They reinforce your worth. They show you are good enough; no one can take that away.

Get Help to Overcome Self-Doubt

The belief that you're not good enough comes from somewhere. Oftentimes, it's from something in your past: a person or an incident triggered the feeling. You developed a sense that something was missing—you didn't have the right background, social status, or family; you didn't have the physical attributes, money, or education.

After all that, it's hard to be fearless alone, to see the truth that you are good enough. If you're particularly prone to self-doubt, find an accountability partner—a trusted friend (or friends) with whom you can share your feelings. The right people can help you assess your abilities and interrupt your habit of senselessly beating yourself up. Kind and strong people will advocate for you and will probably share the same doubts about themselves. Hiring a coach might be a good choice if you need solutions—including a plan to create positive change for yourself, focusing on your talents, gifts, and assets.

In the meantime, advocate for yourself. To start, bust through some of your self-doubts:

- Recall past achievements.
- Don't compare or compete with others.
- Take a sincere interest in others (fear loves to focus solely on you).
- Be mindful of and compassionate toward yourself and oppose your inner bully.
- See vulnerability as a superpower.

A Word on Vulnerability

Being at your most vulnerable is where you may find some of your greatest strengths, skills, values, and meaning. Embrace it rather than fight it or try to pretend you're invincible and perfect in every way. In doing so, you may become the next iteration of yourself.

Think about it:

We are all always vulnerable.
Living makes us vulnerable.
Relationships make us vulnerable.
Work makes us vulnerable.

Creativity and innovation make us vulnerable.

Leading makes us vulnerable.

Our inner critic makes us vulnerable.

Our true state of being is good enough, which is high praise because we are each a perfect and unique energy force, a human being full of potential. That's the truth. When you test it, you'll see it's true, and others will see and feel it with you.

Let me leave you with one deeply transformative exercise.

Exercise: Repeat After Me

Speak these words aloud several times during your day: when you're alone, at work, exercising, shopping, or facing yourself in the mirror: "I am good enough. I am good enough. I Am Good Enough." Sing them, paint them, send yourself emails. See what it does for you.

12

The Fear of Change

Nothing in life is to be feared; it is only to be understood.
Now is the time to understand more so that we may fear less.

– Marie Curie

What I love most about change is that it is always ready for you. You don't need to book an appointment for change in advance. It's never sold out. The shelves are fully stocked with change. You don't need to take a number and wait in line. Change is abundant and immediately available to you whenever you need and want it. It does come through.

And yet . . .

In your mind, draw a circle with the words "fear of change" as if on a blank sheet of paper; draw imaginary lines from that circle, like spokes of a bicycle wheel, and label them: "fear of rejection," "fear of not being good enough," "fear of the unknown," "fear of success," "fear of failure," "fear of trying something new," "fear of not trying," "fear of bullying," and whatever other fear comes to mind. (I could write a whole book on the fear of failure and the fear of success! Look to the resource section at michaelfeeleylifecoach.com/bonus for some helpful information.)

Notice that the fear of change is the nucleus connected to all other fears. You can jump these fear lines, going back and forth between them like a shuttle bus from one stop to another.

Now, my intent in highlighting fear is not to pull you into negativity but to be scientific about the structure of the fears we all experience. It all comes down to the fear of change (uncertainty, entering the great unknown) because you're hard-wired to seek out the predictable. It's perfectly natural to avoid the unfamiliar. That's what kept your ancestors safe. But now, hard wiring isn't keeping you safe from saber-toothed tigers lurking in the bushes; it's preventing you from leading a more satisfying life.

Why Do You Fear Change?

One way to slow down or stop the shuttling back and forth between change-related fears is to name what you're afraid of. "I'm scared because _____."

Naming the fear helps, particularly when you share it with a friend or two willing to serve as a sounding board because it's out in the open. You said it. It's real. Now, others can help you understand and solve it.

If you're afraid to change, to leave your comfort zone, to try something different, consider the possibility that your fear is bound up in the possibility of failing or even succeeding. Yes, you can fear success. What will you do if you're successful and don't count on it? How will you deal with success; how will you view yourself and others?

Maybe you get the job offer you worked tirelessly to achieve, and boom, you fear you're not good enough. That's what's coming up. You dive right into resistance and believe you fooled everyone who interviewed you. If you accept the job, they'll quickly see you're a fake, an imposter. *Say no, don't humiliate yourself.*

See how fear trickles down from the fear of change to multiple other fears? So, name these fears, call them out, and refocus on the truth.

Use Fear to Your Advantage

There is often goodness in your fear; take advantage of it. Fear might mean not settling for similar, unstable, and unfulfilling things; it might lead you to be wise and innovative in the face of adversity and to see what's possible and beneficial to you.

You may not see it at first. Keep looking and keep moving forward.

I didn't see change as a colossal gift when I lost my headhunting job, but it was. It was my way out of corporate captivity and relentless stress, competition, and demands for profit that were actively draining the life out of me. I had spent years in this system making money and winning at any expense, and the return was ruining my precious physical and mental health and happiness.

Rather than sit frozen in worry, my decision to do something in the face of change immediately catalyzed a shift. When I committed to getting out of fear and doing the work required to land a new opportunity, I started making better choices, and my fear lessened. Inspiration and creativity arose.

You can start small, as I did: Change your morning routine, try a new hobby, or explore a different neighborhood. Then, practice controlled discomfort by intentionally putting yourself in slightly uncomfortable but safe situations to build resilience.

Spend time journaling your fears. Write about what specifically scares you about change, then break down the fears into realistic vs. imagined.

Build a support system made up of people who've navigated similar changes; create a change toolkit with reliable methods that help you feel grounded (meditation, exercise, talking to a friend). The key is gradual exposure rather than forcing dramatic changes.

Choice, change, and commitment all work together at different times. It's hard to pinpoint which of these three components leads and which one follows. It's a little like the question— which came first, the chicken or the egg?

What is clear, however, is that we all struggle with fear, and sometimes, we use that fear to conveniently stop us from acting and doing the work we're meant to do. Don't sabotage yourself and let resistance win by doing nothing except screwing up your opportunity for happiness and success. Don't hold back or keep yourself small. "I can't" is just as powerful an excuse as "I won't" change.

But if you do the work, show up, and produce with courage, clarity, and purpose, change will help you overcome fear.

Yes, there is a fear of change and a confidence to change. You can flourish by letting go and embracing uncertainty. Hope will become your North Star. Faith in your dreams, vision, and values will allow you to get your bearings. It will serve as your compass in uncertain times and lead you safely home to where you're meant to be.

PART III:
AN ACHIEVABLE PLAN

13

Stay or Go

———

There are three constants in life: change, choice, and principles.

—Stephen Covey

Thus far, we've talked about the mindset you need to adopt when you reach a crossroads in your career and the skills, values, and dreams you need to connect with before you enter uncharted territory. We've addressed the fears you'll no doubt meet on your journey and how to recognize them for what they are (resistance or reality checks). Now it's time to create a plan and make some key decisions so you can get what you want and not be tossed around by circumstances.

But first, we need a story that will lead us to our next step...

I've said it before, and I'll say it again: I loved my work as a headhunter, filling jobs, developing business, and connecting to the needs and wishes of clients and candidates.

In my years of staffing, one manager understood my work and offered encouragement in our meetings. Others lived indifferently behind the title of "Manager." They demanded things they could never do themselves. Unable to inspire, lazier than a piece of sod, they were fond of letting me know, "You are only as good as your last placement... (but keep working so I can pay my mortgage)."

When I first met Mittens (or so we'll call her), she told me she wanted to meet all my clients and set up personal meetings as soon as possible. She also wanted me to start and finish my day in the office. I'm not good at being told what to do, like an organ grinder's monkey on a leash. I was a hard worker and a producer, and I liked my freedom in my work.

A big part of the work I did was setting up early morning meetings with the HR person I was courting. Sometimes, I was up at four a.m. so I could get dressed and bring coffee from their favorite coffee shop before our five or six a.m. meeting. These meetings gave us time to get to know each other without interruptions and for me to learn more about the company.

Similarly, at the end of the day, if I had the chance to take someone out for drinks to build connections and business, I jumped at it. Sometimes, I'd start cold calling a building, working my way from the top all the way down to the lobby, office by office.

This approach to client acquisition and management worked well for me, yet it conflicted with the new rule of starting and ending each day at headquarters.

I told Mittens she could meet me at these appointments, knowing she never would take me up on the invitation. Getting into a crowded subway early in the morning was too much of a hassle for her. As a "compromise," Mittens insisted I return after the early-morning meetings to appear in the office.

I complained to my old manager about her rules, and he said, "Deal with it."

Mittens, who didn't like my attitude, continuously patronized me and my work. Shaking her head, she'd say, "What am I going to do with you, Michael?" And yet, I was producing—building great clients and making good placements and money.

The division's owners and department heads gathered around me and said flat out, "You have too much power. You bring in top clients, and then you fill the jobs. You shouldn't be allowed to approve the candidates; that's not how it works. You're in outside sales. You should flip the client to other people once you get them."

I explained that it didn't seem right to work so hard to gain a client's trust, learn what they want, and then hand them over to someone else when they know nothing about the person or company.

Instead of seeing things my way, they wanted me to quit so they could take over. They made increasing demands on my production to help me along with that decision. The work I so loved became unbearable. I knew I had to find a new job.

One week, I brought in seven new clients. Still, Mittens insulted me. She wanted me to feel like a failure, to think I was not good enough, which was impossible. I had confidence in myself, and my results backed it up. People watched what was happening. Some had great compassion for me, and that helped me get through my most strenuous, hateful days.

Mittens and company resented my success instead of seeing it as a tribute to them.

Maybe you can relate. Your success at a company makes others feel less. They fear you, so they try to control you, to make you feel unworthy and less successful.

Nearly everything they say to you is unkind. It is decidedly not meant to be positive feedback to help and inspire. They gang up on you. Your whole work experience has become an exhausting, painful, and valuable lesson: the corporate profit hound chooses to control and humiliate their workers who were good at playing the game and bringing home the financial trophies.

Don't give up. After several weeks of this abuse, I found a job I liked with a company that said, "With numbers and clients like this, you can do whatever you want and more." Things can turn around for you, too.

But before you even ask if you should stay in your current work situation or go, let me say this: never let anyone control and humiliate you. Ever! No person or job is worth lessening yourself or exploiting your gifts and values. It's never about money. It's about you not selling yourself out or tolerating contempt and disrespect. Consider this my disclaimer.

You Have a Choice to Make

Before putting together a tangible plan from which to work, you need to know where you're going. When deciding whether you'll stay at your current job or find something new, ask yourself these questions: can I fix what is wrong at work; do I even want to try?

People choose to stay in their present jobs for various reasons. Still, it's often money and familiarity—they don't want to deal with the change of writing a new resume, looking for work, and interviewing. The process seems too much until they are emotionally and physically ready for a specific job change and search, which is perfectly understandable.

If that's you, I passionately encourage you to be ready for an immediate change in case it happens. Have your resume updated and ready to go, as well as three to five current impeccable references. Always look around, be informed, and see what's available and happening in your arena and in the marketplace. Now is the best time to look for a new job, even when you're happy. Don't be a lazy Mittens in this regard.

When you choose to stay in your current role, you embark on a journey of self-reflection (at least you should). I'll guide you through the process of creating the opportunity for you to excel in your current position, leading to a more fulfilling work life. It will also grow you if you wind up leaving after all.

By examining and reassessing the details, facts, and emotions related to your daily tasks and responsibilities and pausing long enough to see them in a new light, you can refresh, reset, and rejuvenate yourself and your role. Keep what works well, release what doesn't, and change where you can improve. It's basic addition and subtraction.

Stop blaming others for your unhappiness, especially if you're being overlooked for raises or promotions, even if you have a narcissistic boss who likes holding you back. Remove any "You stop me from... when will you see my value... things would be different if..." kind of talk. Only truthful self-assessment leads to positive change.

To be clear, you might try hard to make things work, but it may also be time to stop walking uphill, backward, with a blindfold over your eyes and one leg tied around your neck.

So, What Do You Really Want?

Are you scratching your head about whether to stay or go? Then it may be time to ask yourself some questions and pay attention to what immediately pops up in response.

> **Exercise: The Truth of Your Current Position**
>
> 1. How respected do you feel at work?
>
> 2. How sincerely expressed at work are you?
>
> 3. How motivated are you by your work; does it create a change you are passionate about?
>
> 4. How much are you growing and making an impact, a difference, and contributions to the well-being of others?

5. What's missing that you want to add, and what do you want to remove or alter?

What's the first thing that comes to your mind? Write it down. Speak it out loud and make it real so you can't take it back. No doubt, your answer depends on how happy you are with your work or not.

At the very least, you're flirting with leaving. You wouldn't be reading this book if you weren't. So, if you do decide to go and look for different work, you've got another set of questions to consider.

Exercise: Create Your Master List of Requirements

1. What will I accept and not accept?

2. What is the yes and no for my next position?

3. What must I have? What's a deal-breaker?

4. What salary do I need?

5. What are the health and vacation benefits?

6. Where do I want to live, and what is the cost of living there?

7. What is my ideal role: position, title, and responsibilities?

8. What is the growth potential?

9. Who will I be working with?

10. How does the company ensure everyone is heard, respected, and has a fair chance to succeed?

11. What will my quality of life be like in this job?

12. Will I live in or out of integrity if I do this work?

Now that you've made this master list, prioritize and rank what comes first, second, third, and so on in order of importance. What's number one—what do you want most on your list?

Consider these questions and conduct thorough research on companies, people, and career opportunities. Even if you decide to stay where you are, you can use these questions to reassess your present job, make changes, reset and renew yourself, or accept what you have and keep working as you are.

It's exciting to know that change is possible. There are many hopeful and gratifying choices and possibilities, so remain calm.

You Think You Want to Stay

Renewing yourself is like coming out of hibernation, the process an animal or plant goes through after being dormant all winter. It's a journey of awakening to what you genuinely want.

You want to remember and revive the gratitude you felt in your heart those first days and weeks on the job. It shouldn't be a burden or a source of fear. You're simply trying to find love for your work once again.

It's not simply about the people and situations around you. Think about how you showed up on your first day at work. Start fresh. Show up untarnished, without petty self-judgment—with sincere energy and commitment.

- How will you show up from this day forward?

- How will you dress and act?

- Will you reorganize your desk?

- Will you change how you speak to those around you?

- How can you get to know your fellow workers better; how can you be more helpful?

Why not meet with your boss: ask where you can improve, and add what you plan on doing? Create the change you want and see how it affects you and the people around you.

(Simultaneously, you should keep your options open and explore new job opportunities in the same company or outside.)

You'll have new energy and hunger for your work when you actively move forward. There will be excitement, curiosity, and the kind of inspiration you felt when you first got your job. You'll drive to clean things up in your life: plan, improve, and get back on track—not simply go through the minimal motions. Your self-respect and pride, stature, significance, and dignity will be renewed.

The enjoyable part of this awakening is that you have the power to start fresh and escape the miserable feeling of being hemmed in or bored to distraction.

I'm confident you can pull yourself out of your rut and find a way (or twenty ways) to revive yourself and the work you love.

It's Definitely Goodbye for You

Maybe you feel it in your bones and in your heart. It's time to reinvest in yourself and recognize all you have to offer, becoming an asset, not an afterthought. You know you want to go; that's all there is to it.

Bye-bye, old position. Hello, new adventure. I'll say it again with joy: all your skills are transferable. They will work wherever you go, even in a different line of work. So, welcome back!

Let's start with that unique value you offer. Where do people count on you in and outside of work? How do they rely on you; why do they respect you; what do they desperately need from you daily? These are tributes you do not want to overlook. They should pop into your head before anything else because you must be grounded before marching into the unknown.

You'll want to head in a good direction, not just go from bad to worse, which is where impulsivity often lands you. So, spend time imagining what you'll do and where you'll do it.

Maybe it's time to relocate. Perhaps it's time to do what you always wanted to do—what you've dreamt about. Anything and everything is possible, particularly when you're clear on your transferable skills, gifts, and talents.

If the very idea brings up fear—makes you feel stuck, unable, and not ready to move for legitimate reasons, that's OK. That's why we covered the need to face your fears before you make a plan. Even that is a positive step toward change.

Timing is important, but for now, let's come back to the miracle of possibilities. Say it out loud, one phrase after the other:

I'm possible.

I'm capable.

I can.

I want to.

I will.

Here I go.

Remember, change is ready for you at any time.

Sure, there will be some fear, doubt, and pressure. That's natural. But more significant is the sense of relief and gratitude it brings, the many options you can explore because you have a way to get unstuck.

It's not easy to know what you want. Sometimes, you have to come at it from another direction and consider what you don't want. Here's one way to go about it...

Exercise: What You Do/Don't Want

Take a piece of paper and fold it in half. On one side, write down what you want; on the other, what you don't. (You can do the same with the advantages and disadvantages of staying.) Be spontaneous; write the things that immediately come to mind.

Answering these questions will help you clarify:

1. What do I want to do?

2. Why do I want this?

3. What don't I want?

4. Why don't I want this?

And the fireworks question:

5. What would I do if I lost my job tomorrow (and I sincerely hope you do not)?

Ninety percent of the people I coach have an answer right away. "I'd teach tap and ballroom dancing... I'd write a book... travel... open my own gardening business... renovate homes and resell them... take piano lessons... learn French and Italian... get a divorce and find true love... throw a BIG party... get to know myself." All real answers from real people.

Reimagining yourself takes work and courage, so please do it carefully despite the pressure and concerns. (If you need help celebrating the opportunity to choose, you'll find "Freedom of

Choice – Your Greatest Gift" at michaelfeeleylifecoach.com/ bonus.)

It's A New Day

Every day is a clean slate, a chance for you to say, "Let's begin again." Begin again to live, work on a project you love, create, innovate, reset, rejuvenate, and release what holds you back.

It can be about a title, salary, degree, and various accolades. But it's often something far deeper and more meaningful. It's about being the best at your work and pouring your whole self into whatever you do, be it work, job, career, vocation, or passionate dream.

I often quote these inspiring words of Martin Luther King, Jr. because I love them! They express a key component of serving others no matter what kind of work you do and the choice to do your very best:

> If it falls your lot to be a street sweeper, sweep streets like Michelangelo painted pictures, sweep streets like Beethoven composed music, sweep streets like Leontyne Price sang before the Metropolitan Opera. Sweep streets like Shakespeare wrote poetry. Sweep streets so well that all the hosts of heaven and earth will have to pause and say: "Here lived a great street sweeper who did his job well."

> If you can't be a pine at the top of the hill, be a shrub in the valley. Be the best little shrub on the side of the hill... If you can't be a highway, be a trail. If you can't be a sun, be a star. For it isn't by size that you win or fail. Be the best of whatever you are.

Every day, you are presented with the profound possibility of contributing to something greater than yourself—from the work immediately in front of you to the world at large. This journey of self-discovery is not simply a step; it's a leap in your pursuit of passion and excellence, in giving out your best work.

Reach for what you want because you can. Your best is not just valuable; it's essential. All your skills and training, talents, gifts, knowledge, life experience, passions, dreams, and heart are not just valuable but necessary. Don't be an imitation of anyone else. Be the real you. The world eagerly awaits your unique contribution and goodness. Please do not keep people waiting.

14

Choose to Become More You

———

Live! Live the wonderful life that is in you! Let nothing be lost upon you.
Be always searching for new sensations. Be unafraid of nothing.

—Oscar Wilde

Disruption at any age is painful, but the need for security, good health, and emotional and financial balance becomes a priority as you mature, which makes stepping away from the security of such things more difficult. You may not see it now, but a career change can be a gift, no matter how badly wrapped. It allows you to focus, recenter, and rebalance yourself. It's a transformational opportunity.

For example, when I stepped away from the corporate pressure:

I began to experience new emotions. One morning, I saw a red cardinal standing in the sunlight on gray pebbles in the driveway. I stood there for a long time, captivated by the sheer beauty and simplicity before me... and I was happy. I felt something for the first time in years; for far too long, I had been shut down, too focused on producing revenue and numbing myself. At last, my heart could open to the wonder of the world around me.

My mind worked better. It was calmer, clearer, more flexible, and open. My vocabulary was growing or, rather, coming back. For so long, I had relied on words with little meaning. "Awesome... cool... WOW!... no kidding... checking in... touching base... later."

I found myself reading again. I read all the books by Martha Beck, Seth Godin, Libby Gill, Deepak Chopra, and Byron Katie. They were books about finding your destiny and value, getting unstuck, and discovering your true self; I couldn't put them down. I learned new things about myself and what was stopping me from having the life I most wanted. If there were exercises to do, I did them all. I dug deep into myself and questioned who I was and how I lived.

I enjoyed hours of intense, joyful self-exploration and experienced positive, invigorating change.

My health began to improve. I slept better, ate better (not fast at my desk), lost weight, and started singing aloud. I had pushed myself hard to succeed—I met every task the company set and bought into selling myself out. So much of my potential was restricted, and I ran on empty. All my choices, mind you, but nonetheless, I felt the effects of not operating under my values.

Oh, the choices I made to stay in a career that had ceased to be good for me. I wasn't burned out; I was misusing myself. I had too much, and I kept acquiring more. I regret how selfish and wasteful I was. It didn't balance well with my care for people and the profound joy I felt helping them find temporary or permanent jobs.

Perhaps you'll see, as I did, that one of the most valuable things you can do is focus on how much you really need to live. Beyond basic human needs, what do you really need to feel complete (finances, home, food, clothing, even friends)? It's not about deprivation or suffering but rather a call to be sensible and wise about your life choices. The quality of your life should matter most—and it should serve as the filter to evaluate it all.

Making Better Choices

The decisions we make create our lives. When you study the results of your choices, conscious or otherwise, you may find you have betrayed many of your core values, which have left you feeling depleted or otherwise unhappy.

In the interest of making your next chapter far more fulfilling, begin to make new and better choices:

- Consciously slow down; work on being patient, genuine, caring, and giving.

- Keep your ego in check. Consider the needs of those around you, including friends and family.

- Be present in all you do. Don't leap around in twenty different directions.

- Focus on gratitude for your life and the world around you.

- Recognize and prioritize your core values.

- Find out exactly what you want to do and where you want to go, then build a doable plan to get there.

And don't forget self-care. Value *yourself;* treat yourself with respect, kindness, and love, and you'll become far more confident, generous, positive, vibrant, alert, and alive. In short, you'll feel better.

Committing to making better choices will help you know and stay true to yourself; it will change the way you look at potential opportunities. It will also allow you to be the same everywhere you go—at home, work, with friends. You'll live your life rather than play a game.

The Right Opportunity Will Emerge

If finding the right opportunity seems daunting, take heart: sometimes, your true calling finds you. Once you discover your passion and values and begin to make better choices, the puzzle pieces have a way of working themselves into place.

For me, it was the friend who suggested life coaching. She knew I'd look up every reference I could find to see if it was right for me, and I did. The fear of change started to fade away when I saw how this career could feed my sense of purpose. Since it requires service, giving, caring, and helping—the foundation of who I am—I knew I could thrive. I evaluated my options and planned new action steps. This action began with sending emails to specific heads of coach training programs and coaches with highly successful businesses, asking to speak with them. They all responded cheerfully, generously, and openly, which made me love the industry even more.

Yes, it was still a lot of work and education (which continues to this day). I had to ask for what I wanted and promote myself. I had to build a whole new business and career as a Life, Career, and Change Coach, which included offering my services free of charge to get the initial experience and testimonials. But it was worth it. Not only did it become profitable, but it also became the career I love—all because someone spoke direction into my life.

That's just one of the ways the right opportunity may find you.

Get out there and try new experiences, volunteer, get involved in your community, join a club or professional organization, and surround yourself with positive people. There is something to the saying, "In the right place at the right time." You just might have the chance to see for yourself.

Calling In Backup

You can absolutely discover yourself and find the career that suits you best. It's not impossible, though it may take a bit of digging and a few changes. It may take some time. But sometimes, you find yourself stuck. Sometimes, you need another vantage point to see the qualities and emotions you honestly want in life—to consider what's working and what's not.

That's where coaching comes in.

People look to a coach to figure out what to do with their lives, work, transitions, careers, and much more. They're people who are not ready to quit at fifty-plus years (or well into their eighties, for that matter). And they're looking for guidance in their plan of attack.

Coaches are all about helping you live your "true self." What does that mean?

In his essay, "How to Tell the Difference Between Your True Self and Your Everyday Self," Deepak Chopra, M.D., scholar and author, writes:

> The true self isn't a familiar term to most people, although it is close to what religion calls your soul, the purest part of your-self... the trick is distinguishing what is your true self and what is not... There are moments when you feel secure, accepted, peaceful, and certain. At these moments, you're experiencing your true self. True is certain and clear. Every day leads to con-fusion. The true self is driven by a deep sense of truth. The everyday self is driven by ego, the unending demand of 'I,' Me, Mine.

In essence, a coach helps you pinpoint the truth and facts about yourself that can then be easily transitioned into your life and work. There are no tricks; no faking, and simple honesty and openness are all it takes.

Visioning

We've touched on understanding what an ideal outcome would look like for you. If you're still unsure of the details or having trouble keeping the end goal in sight, I present to you... visioning.

Visioning is a powerful tool that helps you visualize your professional future. Basically, you create a meaningful and fulfilling life that suits you to a tee. And you do so in such a way that you can see, taste, and smell it—to feel the joy and happiness well before you experience the actual success. That motivates you to take the essential steps to get from where you are to where you want to be.

It's a catalyst for personal growth.

Visioning is not a magical woo-woo concept; it's a call to action. It's a scientific process showing how your future vision impacts your behavior and choices. That's why companies and governments use it to set goals, solve problems, and offer special services and products.

You can use it to shape your own future. The work is intense, fun, detailed, thorough, and thrilling. And your commitment to it is crucial.

> **Exercise: Visioning**
> Look into the future, starting with four weeks from today. Be scientific as you gather data and use all your senses—and please write it down.

1. What do you see?

2. What do you hear?

3. What do you smell, taste, and touch?

4. Who are the people you're connected to?

5. Where is this place, and what are you doing so this vision will become natural, and you can thrive and feel at home?

Here's an example:

I always loved the idea of relocating, living, and working in another place and culture, and Paris is one of those dream destinations. Thus, the following...

I'm in Paris, and my office is across the Seine, near the Louvre Museum. The lobby is busy with people climbing the steps to other floors and taking glass elevators upwards. Brilliant sunlight streams into the entrance, and fresh white calla lilies are in a large, frosted glass vase on the circular wooden lobby desk.

My office is on the third floor. The modern reception area has painted sage-colored walls, light gray carpet, natural wood paneling, and a colorful Chagall painting. I hear soft piano music playing and smell lavender's gentle, pleasant scent—so French.

I wear a navy blue pin-stripe suit and a light blue open-collared shirt. I carry a black leather envelope briefcase and feel deeply happy and hopeful about my fresh start as a CXO - Chief Experience Officer.

My boss is a renaissance woman who believes that trusting the people she works with brings out their best. She is practical and creative with meta-thinking in realistic and adventurous directions. She's building a team of innovators in environmental change, especially in the hospitality industry of travel, hotels, and rental homes. They are unafraid to try and fail and do it again because that is where progress and success come from. The team is diverse. Six people from different cultures, ages, and experiences who are passionate about their work and count on others as they build valuable and generous possibilities for people—for humanity.

I'm thrilled to begin this fresh start at seventy-two with a lifetime of skills and experience. I get to do work I love as the CXO - Chief Experience Officer: learn new things, serve other people, solve problems, and help us all live good lives daily to ensure the future of our world.

See what I mean about envisioning the vital details of your future change, happiness, and success? It's important because what you want, imagine, and send out to the universe does come back to you. It's the law of attraction. Send out negativity, and you will get it back. It's also called karma.

Once you've got the details, then you can begin to plan.

Create a Change Plan

Look around, and you'll see change everywhere: day turns to night, fruit ripens, and your body's cells change every second and fully replace themselves in seven years. You change clothes for an occasion and change lanes when you drive. When it comes to permanent and lasting change, you start by changing how you see and think about the world.

Again, change is scary. You have fears, but you do not have to obey them. That's why you need to create a plan to minimize the fear and ensure the right outcome.

Exercise: Create a Change Plan

Write down three things you want to change in your life and work (these days, work and life tend to overlap more than ever).

1.

2.

3.

Congratulations. You just stepped into *change*. It's on paper, so it's real, and it came from you.

Next, pick one of the three items you wrote down and answer these two questions:

1. Why is this change important to you?

2. What will happen when you achieve this change?

Finally, build your plan.

If you're looking to change jobs, it might look something like this:

1. What will you do first? (Make a list of five to ten companies you hunger to work at. You'll research them and see what openings they have.)

2. When will you do it? (Give yourself a deadline. If it's Monday, give yourself five hours to complete it, start at nine a.m. and finish by two p.m.)

3. How achievable is it? (This means it's entirely possible to thoroughly research five to ten companies and their associated job openings in a span of five hours. If not, you'll need to revisit the first two steps.)

4. How will you hold yourself accountable? (You need a way to confirm you met your deadline. You might include your partner or a friend to hold you accountable—and lavish praise on you at two p.m. when you reach the goal.)

Don't give yourself orders. It's time to be good to yourself and celebrate coming this far. Change is a process. It only takes your time and commitment, and you can give both.

Watch out for Resistance. Your inner bully is always hunting for you, so meet him at the door and say you're full up and closed.

Now that you have the basic idea of how to examine and achieve your desired change, let's get into action.

15

Creating Your Plan of Action

Can anything be sadder than work left unfinished? Yes, work never done.
—**Christina Rossetti**

Dreams do not come true without miles of hard work, heartbreak, frustration, and a steadily growing self-confidence in your skills. Nor does it happen without an actionable plan.

As you know, I aspired to be a professional actor and singer in New York City. I had a meticulously crafted plan, complete with the steps I needed to take. This plan was rigorously tested and found effective throughout high school, college, and my move to New York City, where the dream came true. I did the same thing with each subsequent "act" (as a headhunter and coach).

You need your own Plan of Action (POA), whether your goal is to completely switch careers or improve your current work environment. Nothing will happen without it. A POA is a goal and actionable steps to achieve it. It also entails loads of hope, creativity, enthusiasm, and the tenacity to show up and do the demanding work to get what you want.

Defining your POA is a pivotal step as you shift your career. You will need to be precise, listen to yourself, and get back to the basics of what you want and how you will achieve it.

Exercise: Big Picture Plan of Action

Take a pen and paper and write down what you want and what actions you can take to get it. Write freestyle without judging yourself or your words. Be sloppy and open. See what comes up spontaneously.

If you need some ideas, most plans cover the following:

1. What do you want? (Industry – Title - Location)

2. Marketing (Resume - Cover Letter - Online Profile)

3. Research (Job Boards - Social Media – Companies - People)

4. Networking (People You Know - Online Connections - Building Relationships)

5. Interviewing (Be Yourself - Share Your Skills - Ask Questions - Assess the Company and People)

6. Be organized and motivated (Keep Track of Work Sent Out - Follow Up on Possibilities)

7. Negotiate (Ask for What You Want - Get the Offer – Decide: Is This What You Want)

> Map it all out: what, when, where, and why (which may include working for yourself and running your own business). It should include everything you need to get you on your feet with resources, finances, services, and products.

Knowing what you want is the first giant step to getting the work that will light you up.

Once you have a better idea of what you want, you can gather more details. This starts with figuring out what's a go and what's a no-go. What's a "Hell, yes!" and what's a deal breaker.

Acceptable vs. Unacceptable

It's time to redefine the norms for 50-, 60-, 70-, and 80-year-olds in careers, jobs, and work. The existing rules can feel restrictive and unkind as you age, but you can change them and create new ones that better suit your aspirations and abilities.

To explore this further, create a list of what you will accept and what is unacceptable as you consider the work you want to do. You have standards and values for both life and work. Chances are good; they're one and the same, but that's for you to decide as you work things out.

Maybe you need a certain salary. You may love the idea of a given position. Still, you'll need to walk away or renegotiate if it doesn't fall within your acceptable range. Unacceptable often rules, and that is perfectly OK. "This is unacceptable." They are powerful, decisive words, usually based on integrity and work ethics.

Maybe excessive paperwork is a no-go, mandatory unpaid overtime, or that you be available twenty-four hours a day, including weekends. Working hours need to suit you. What hours will be acceptable? Put that on your acceptable vs. unacceptable list.

You may need a specific title to work remotely and the ability to dress casually (or professionally). You may want a boss who gives you the freedom to do your work and produce without being micromanaged and consistently pulled into meetings where very little happens.

Exercise: A Deeper Go-No-Go

Your values will set the stage for what you're looking for in a company:

1. What do I need and want in a career? What is acceptable?

2. What's an absolute deal breaker for me?

3. Where might I compromise on what I need and want while still respecting myself?

4. What values must be aligned for me to fit?

In light of your values, consider a company's reputation:

5. What does their positive and negative feedback look like on social media?

6. How do their services and products affect others?

7. What is the work atmosphere and culture like?

8. How are people treated?

If you don't like what you see, consider it a red flag (and unacceptable).

Now, list the job requirements you will need in no uncertain terms:

9. Salary:

10. Benefits:

11. Location:

12. Growth possibilities:

To further fill out your list:

13. Name your top five must-haves, and then prioritize them.

14. Name your top five "no way - no deal."

Knowing what is acceptable and not acceptable is vital to finding a job that suits you. You'll need to be clear about this at your present job and when looking for other work (or building that new career). And trust your gut feeling from the moment you enter a given workspace. (We'll talk more about the interview process in another chapter.)

Resources for Developing a Plan of Action

You have a wealth of resources to help you develop your plan of action. You can hire a career coach or read self-help books. (You can also check out my brainstorming resource at michaelfeeleylifecoach.com/bonus.)

Even small steps can have a great impact. Read want ads and job postings in newspapers, job boards, or company websites; attend job fairs; meet with headhunters; or simply find someone who believes in you, sticks with you, and cares about what it is you need and want. (See the next section for more details.)

We've already touched on researching companies, but it's another great option. Learn all you can. Meet and connect with people who work at the companies you're interested in. Get wildly creative and send letters asking for what you want—a job interview for a specific job in a special department for a particular person. Again, this can all be listed as task items in your plan.

From there, you can send your resume, notes (hand-delivered), and emails; find people you know who can introduce you to the firm or individuals who work there, all to help you get what you want. An unexpected interview or job lead may pop up. Once you take the first step, you can spot the next two or three things you'll need to do. Once you work on those things, the next ten will make themselves apparent, and just like that, you have yourself a workable plan.

Job Finding Dance Steps

If you're looking for specifics, here are the typical dance steps for finding a job or opportunity to go after:

1. Look at job boards such as Indeed, Glassdoor, CareerBuilder, U.S. News Job Search, and Monster to see what positions are open.

2. Choose five companies and five people you'd kill to work for and then research the life out of them. Learn all you can.

3. Research remote jobs—flexible jobs—freelancers—work from home. There are amazing sites for mature workers because many companies value experienced workers: AARP—Work at Home—New Solutions—Vintage Experts.

4. Reach out to people you know and ask for help. Hopefully, you have been building relationships with the people in your social media databases, not just connecting for the number of "likes" and "followers." Networking with the right people is essential when looking for a job.

5. Find a real person to contact. Get the name of the person hiring, including the first and last name (make sure to spell them correctly), and start building a relationship. Sometimes you can't get the name, I know, but do your best. Great letters can always be written with these words: "To Whom It May Concern."

Side note: I once earned a client because I spelled her name correctly, Dianne, not Diane. She called me, set up an interview, and gave me work because she said that rare was the person who cared enough to know how to spell someone's name. It does matter; it's a sign of respect.

6. Go to LinkedIn, visit the company's "About" pages, and Google away to find the right people and see how you're related. Who do you both know? What do you have in common? Maybe you went to the same school and have the same interests and goals.

7. Learn about the company to create relevant interest in yourself and prepare for interviews. Set yourself up to earn a job or, when a job opens up, to be considered immediately. Don't follow the "formula herd" by sending out the same boring letters and going through the motions.

All that aside, here's my best career advice: relationships and creativity matter. Reach out to your connections, no matter how well you know them. Network and be innovative even if you think companies and people don't have a job opening. You never know.

Asking Should Be Part of Your Plan

There are abundant and unlimited opportunities, but sometimes you must ask. It works, but it also takes practice; so, practice...

To start, remind yourself that you're skilled. You have the credentials, experience, and success that people need and are looking for. You need to inform them of your presence and get in front of them by stepping outside the masses. Show them you love the work and have the right energy, gratitude, and an open heart.

Now, what is one thing you want to ask for, and why? Once you name it, immediately create the first simple step to make it happen. Build another step the next day and every day after so you're active and can be proud of your work. You're a professional, not an amateur or a dabbler.

Don't sit around and wait for HR to pick up the phone and call you about your resume. Make things happen for you. And don't be afraid to ask.

Be Flexible with Your Plan

You are an enterprise—a unique person with precious skills and experience—so treat your job hunt as a business. Take your time. Look at and feel what is happening in the industry you seek to work in. Even though you have a plan, realize that you can work out of sequence. Be flexible, open, and curious.

Maybe you're getting good results and interviews for customer service jobs in website design and development, and you also want to expand into graphic design for promotional materials, eBooks, bonus scripts and products, and surveys.

You can explore industries that do not advertise or start-ups.

You may see something you'd like to move into, even though you're not yet skilled enough to do the job well.

As you interview, you will most likely meet with younger people who have preconceptions of you as a mature person. I mention this because ageism is real, and you should be aware of what you may surprisingly encounter in interviews so you can adjust your approach and tactics and hope to connect with everyone in the best way possible as you look for work.

Having a plan will guide your steps in the right direction. Of course, there are always potential obstacles, so allowing for detours is important. And since your plan is all about showcasing your skills and what you have to offer, let's dive into what that looks like on paper (or the monitor, as the case may be).

16

Write Your Resume

The truth is always exciting. Speak it, then. Life is dull without it.

—Pearl S. Buck

Here we are, at that place most people consider the start of the career-shifting journey. But you know better. You know that identifying and then connecting to your transferable skills, values, and dreams, adjusting your mindset, dealing with the fears that come up in the face of change, and coming up with a flexible plan of action to keep you on task must all come first. Now, even if you decide to stay where you are and do what you can to improve your work environment, having an updated resume will keep your options open and open doors to the next delightful opportunity.

Webster defines a resume as "a summing up; a summary . . . a statement of a job applicant's previous employment experience, education, etc." A resume is also called a CV, from the Latin, *curriculum vitae.* Loosely translated, it means "the course of my life," a definition I much prefer.

A resume tells your story. It's a one-to-two-page document that presents who you are to the outside world. It's a marketing tool, essentially. Its job is to sell and promote you, to get you in the door for the interview. Yes, you are a person, but you're also a product, and people buy the best-advertised product on the market. Your experience and originality are what get homed in on first. Sure, details (the quality and color of the paper, the typeface, and the overall design) are part of the sale. Still, if you ignore what makes you unique, it's into the slush pile you go. So, you want your resume to stand out—to truly showcase your strengths and talents. And it needs to do so in the first twenty seconds.

So, You Hate Writing Resumes

You might feel that writing a resume is akin to doing your taxes. You'll do anything to avoid it. (This could be why you're clinging to a job that no longer serves you.)

Writing a resume touches on two things: **outer blocks** and **inner blocks**.

Outer blocks relate to time, skills, education, and money. They are things that are primarily out of your control. They include how much time will be devoted to your work, what skills are needed, what level of education or experience is required for the job, and how much it pays. (See? There's a reason I had you get clear on your POA, complete with the go-no-go details, before entering the land of resume building.)

Inner blocks include limiting beliefs, uncertainty, judgments, self-doubt, and your inner bully who says, "You're not good enough. Your skills are pathetic and limited. You'll never succeed. There are so many other people better than you."

When you know the blocks and what stops you, you can break through your fears and doubts and tell your bully to go away, "Get lost!" Consciously, you'll choose to make a new and better choice to be free and move forward.

To replace the drudgery mindset with some fun, tell the truth about who you are. List the rich facts and fill in the blanks about your original, talented self.

Remember, it's simply an opportunity to tell your story—who you are and what you do—so your future boss immediately buys into you. The same is true for cover letters (that's coming up, too).

You'll want your resume to be as unique as you are. Trust me, recruiters see thousands of resumes; the ones that catch their eyes are unique and fresh. They reek of confidence and achievements, making the decision easy to pick up the phone and contact the person.

Here's what sets them apart from the others. Consider them your Golden Rules.

Golden Rule #1: Don't Be Generic

First things first: the template for your resume is standard. It should include the company name and location, your title, and the dates of employment (not just years but months). See each job you worked as a headline, then fill in the rest. Be spontaneous; don't judge what you're writing. The goal is to get it down on paper. List what you do, your accomplishments, abilities, and ambitions. Avoid being perfect.

Don't worry about the style. You'll send it to a resume expert (and you must do this to be taken seriously as a professional) who will make it look beautiful. The resume should be no longer than two pages, simple, with clean lines, and easy to read.

No originality, no heart, or mind makes for a poor resume. The use of standard, boring buzzwords kills interest. "Managed . . . responsible for . . . played a key role . . . trained and supervised." (Wake me when you're done.)

I'm not saying don't use these words, but use them once, change them up, and find other adjectives and synonyms to express the importance of your job and skills.

One client I work with is the decision-maker for all financial awards at his firm and throughout their affiliates in the U.S. On his resume, he called himself "The Caretaker of Finances." Now, that's an attention-getter.

Every posted job has specifics, and you will want to adapt yourself accordingly to be seen as a vital, relevant candidate for the open position. I'm not talking about rewriting your resume for every opening, merely adding relevant required skills, highlighting your accomplishments, and shaping it to the company's vision and requirements. It's the same as deciding what to wear to an interview because you want to make a good impression. It's about being what they want and still being who you are, helping them see your value.

Golden Rule #2: Pay Attention to the Energy of Your Words

What kind of energy do you want your resume to have: positive, constructive, and uplifting, or negative, destructive, and dull?

Your resume will impact future employers the moment it is viewed. You want it to be positive because there needs to be an instant connection. That keeps people reading. It should not only inform but also provide a higher impetus to interview you.

Words have power. The words you choose are vital to the success of your resume. The right words will motivate, stimulate, and attract. They build interest and excitement about you and your work.

Here are two examples to illustrate the power of words and how you can create a strong, appealing resume of interest. Which one do you prefer?

The First

1. Managed a staff of eight—"hands-on" visible role.
2. Increased revenue by 25%.
3. Problem solver.
4. Administered $2 million budget.
5. Liaised between management, line personnel, and clients.
6. Maintained office and employee morale.

Certainly, there is nothing wrong with this. The person has solid experience. But what if we brainstorm a little and use more positive words? See if we can make the focus words shift the energy higher to become more profound, exact, expressive, and appealing . . .

The Second

1. Guided and developed a team of eight people, both as a member and teacher.

2. Exceeded anticipated revenue goal by 25%.

3. Adept at solving individual and collective questions, problems, and emergencies.

4. Highly capable of expediting and administering budgets of all sizes.

5. Goodwill ambassador to upper management, fellow employees, and company clients.

6. Fortified and encouraged ethical values, such as mutual respect and commitment, resulting in greater productivity, high team spirit, and a company atmosphere of abundance, vitality, and pride.

Notice the power of choice in people's words when expressing who they are. Let your words lead you. Be a leader with your resume.

People and companies may tell you to leave your emotions at the door. It's not professional to show what you feel; people won't take you seriously if you do. I believe the opposite.

Emotions show character, help build strong teams, and make employees feel authentic, the same person in and out of the job.

Golden Rule #3: Take Command and Take Advantage Too

Your summary is the first thing a prospective employer sees. It's the key that opens your resume. Please take full advantage of it. Exploit this prime space. Be fearless. Entice people with your experience, achievements, and ambitions. Hook them instantly. This is the place to be precise, passionate, creative, and clear about what you want. Get right to the point. Be brief.

Use one or two powerful sentences to express your career goals and aspirations.

Exercise: Sum Yourself Up in One Word

1. Write out a 200-word summary.

2. Then, make it into two simple sentences.

3. And finally, one single word.

This will give you direction, specificity, and confidence in your resume summary.

Note: I'll show you an example of this narrowing process in Chapter 18. Worry not.

Don't be afraid to ask for what you want and tell them why. It's commanding. Many people miss this opportunity or back away from shining their light. (Hello, Resistance.) Go ahead. Dazzle them. There is nothing wrong with a healthy, upfront expression of your worth, and it's damn interesting. This is the time to take charge because it's where leadership shows.

Golden Rule #4: Take Risks, Be Bold, Be Memorable

It's a fact: approximately ninety percent of all applications are submitted online. What will you do with that statistic? Will it discourage or inspire you? How will you go beyond that process, get around it, and add to it? What are you willing to do to be noticed and remembered? What risks are you willing to take to have a company discover you?

Trust yourself. You have nothing to lose and everything to gain by trying new things.

For many years, as an outside sales rep, I had no fear of hand-delivering my proposals. It gave me a chance to visit the locations, observe the tenants and clients coming and going, feel the atmosphere, meet the receptionists, and build relationships with them (the most significant people in the firm). Most importantly, it let the prospective clients know how serious I was about earning their business.

Why not hand-deliver your resume and your proposal of hire? Include a passionate and reasoned note about why you're doing this. "I wanted you to know my sincere, deep desire to do this job and be part of your team. It is crucial to me, so I chose to hand-deliver my resume. I'm eager to meet you and discuss the benefits of working together."

That kind of drive, imagination, innovation, and desire sparks interest. It's the sign of a go-getter, an achiever. Achievers are producers who are creative and have fierce talents to be cherished.

If you really want to gamble and take a risk (and I hope you do), ask if the person hiring is available to speak with you for a few minutes. Why not go all out? You came this far. Be fearless and proud of who you are. If they dislike it, maybe it's not the place for you. Trust me, the right people will take notice of your ingenuity and remember you. That's what matters.

Golden Rule #5: Promote Yourself

Employers look for your achievements and accomplishments. Don't be faint and unclear about yours.

People want to see your value and how it will enhance their company. Everyone—from the file clerk to the executive director—has specific contributions, statistics, recommendations, qualifications, numbers, and revenue to show their success. Tell people what they are. Let them know your worth. Promote your assets. Employers are intensely interested.

And there's no better time than the present to start promoting your worth.

Let's Be Real

Your resume is a chronological history explaining where you worked and what you did (and do). It expresses your true self and should be a near-perfect balance of facts and feelings, outlining your story, "the course of your life."

Everything on your resume needs to be true. Your job title, the companies you worked for, dates of employment (months and years), and even the breaks between jobs (what is not listed) need to be accounted for. And it all needs to be accurate, including grammar and spelling.

Don't forget to proofread. It impacts the initial impression, and background and reference checks will be done to guarantee the facts. Do not be false in any way as you prepare your resume. Be authentic. Be honest.

As William Shakespeare wrote in *Hamlet*, "This above all, to thine own self be true." There's a good reason for that. Suppose you tell the truth, which is attractive to an employer. In that case, you'll likely find yourself in a situation that will allow you to come alive instead of feeling like a fish out of water.

If you're tempted to alter or embellish your resume or change your work history, don't do it. Truth always makes you shine, be it one word, a page, or a volume.

Exercise: Plan or Evaluate Your Resume

If you have yet to create your resume, consider the following questions before you begin. If you are revisiting your resume, evaluate it with these questions in mind:

1. How do I logically and emotionally show who I am on one or two pages?

2. What kind of energy do my words, skills, and background create? (Positive, constructive, exact; or negative, destructive, unclear?)

3. What value or gifts do I bring to a job?

4. How do I want to be seen with my resume?

Your resume is waiting to lead you to your future success. Let it reflect who you truly are inside and out. Include fact and feeling, logic and emotion. Whether you were a doorman or CEO, let your resume reflect your magic. You're greater than you think. Tell your story: I do this, and I'm proud of it.

17

Cover Letter

———

Rarely do we question and then contemplate with determination
what our hearts are calling us to do and to be. I like to frame such
efforts in question form: "What is my job on the planet with a capital J?"
or "What do I care about so much that I would pay to do it?"

–Jon Kabat-Zinn

Some employers want cover letters; others could care less. Ninety-eight percent of the time, you should include a cover letter, so be ready to write one. The standard practice is three to five paragraphs, two hundred fifty to four hundred words.

If you've avoided writing an updated resume, I'm guessing the idea of coming up with a cover letter won't excite you either. But prepare yourself for an attitude upgrade.

I once received a cover letter from a woman who wanted to be a reporter. That was not a position I had ever filled in my headhunting work. Still, the passion and originality of her cover letter (as well as a client recommendation) made me reach out to her immediately for a general interview.

Edwieena was highly articulate, enthusiastic, and captivating. She had top-level computer skills, an English degree, and an extensive travel background. I could tell she had a strong work ethic.

Ask for what you want, and the world comes through in the most interesting and surprising ways: a few days later, as is with the universe, I received a job order to fill as a personal assistant to the editor of one of the top newspapers in New York City. You see, I had something of a reputation for filling nearly impossible jobs.

Even though Edwieena had no experience as a personal assistant, I called her, and we brainstormed about the opportunity this could give her to become the reporter she dreamed of being down the line. She agreed.

I talked with the editor and asked him to trust me, to ignore the lack of experience on her resume, to meet her, and then decide. He agreed. Edwieena and I rehearsed her interview for getting this job, which she absolutely wanted. She saw what I saw and was open to the opportunity. The editor hired her on the spot, and a few years later, she became a reporter. (He also tried to hire me as head of staffing.)

I'm talking about creating opportunities, asking for what you want, planting seeds and waiting for the harvest, and trusting yourself and the world to come through. And it starts with your cover letter.

Uncover Yourself

I like to call cover letters "uncover letters" because they can uncover you from the masses of people applying for the same position. They help people see your value and uniqueness, what you'll contribute if hired, and why they'd want to hire you. So capture their attention.

It's a big step to write about yourself and your worth. You may dislike it because you don't feel comfortable praising yourself. Well, it's time to get over this block. That's probably easier to do when you understand that a cover letter serves a specific purpose in a job application. It's a tool to explain why you're the right fit for the job and to showcase your qualifications.

Like your resume, the purpose of your "confidence letter" (yes, another name I have for a cover letter, indulge me) is to get the interview and then get the job—if you want it after the interview process and offer. See the process and system you're working on?

Let's explore this further and transform it from a daunting task into an opportunity to inspire and engage the reader.

An Opportunity to Shine

Writing a cover letter is not simply a task; it's an opportunity to shine. It's your chance to grab the reader's attention, step out, and demonstrate your full confidence and enthusiasm for the job and the company. Don't go forward if you don't feel that burn and fire. It's a sign that the job may not be the right fit for you. Without a genuine, impelling desire, it's a disservice to both you and the employer to proceed with the application. Don't waste time.

If you choose to go forward, be crystal clear about your purpose in writing and applying for the position. Please do not repeat your resume. You need to craft something different, not reiterate your summary and bullet-point your work history.

This is a motivational letter for the hiring manager and your future boss. So let it rip and express yourself. Be bold and precise with every word and get right to the point.

Strike a sincere pose with your words and qualifications because that will get attention. Write the way you speak. Use your imagination. Be optimistic. Don't be halfhearted or second-rate.

The How-To of Cover Letter Writing

Before you set pen to paper, here's what you are about to do:

- Pitch yourself.
- Uncover your abilities.
- Show your confidence.
- STP: Solve Their Problem. Create a solution to increase your value for a company and fill a need.

- Let people know why *you* are the one even when they can't imagine it.

- Be natural in at least one or two sentences rather than overly formal or contrived. Write what you think and feel, why you like their firm, company, or organization, and why you want to be there.

Think about this: What makes you different from every other person applying with the same expertise and qualifications you have? Fill in their blanks. Lead them.

One way to get started is to remember your first reaction when you heard or read about the job: your exact thoughts, what you said to yourself or told others—the words you used, your gut response. That's your lead. Your focus. Your reason for applying. Don't shy away from these vital things because they're emotional, true, and honest, and your words will affect the reader. (Always keep a pad of paper and pen with you to write things down because I guarantee you will not remember the exact thoughts, words, and emotions you felt. Don't miss the opportunity to be exact, original, and creative.)

Examples:

Take a look at these two choices for confidence letters.
The first:

Re: Customer Service Expert

Dear Ms. Future,

I'm applying for the Customer Service Expert position at Thoroughbred Models, posted on Indeed.com. I'm confident that I can do the job, and you'll see from my attached resume that I'm highly qualified for the position with my six-year tenure as concierge with the Hotel Prestige.

My references are sterling.

My ability to be consistently courteous and helpful, to meet and greet clients in person, and to handle high volumes of telephone inquiries is a deep part of my experience and personal nature. I'm adept at working on busy phone systems and efficiently connecting people to the right person or department. I solve problems quickly and professionally with a level head, even under pressure. I'm entirely comfortable with all of the skills you are searching for. I'm what you're looking for, and it would be an honor to work for your organization because of your professionalism and the quality of work you produce.

Thank you for your consideration. I look forward to meeting with you at your earliest convenience. My contact information is listed below . . .

Note that this meets all the criteria for a cover letter. But look what happens when creativity comes into play...

Enter example two:

Re: Customer Service Expert

Dear Ms. Future,

OK! After hundreds of generic applications—YOU have found your hire. I'm here.

Excellent skills—ready to step into the job—and be fully successful.

I've had one job for six years, running the concierge desk for Hotel Prestige. I'm confident that my experience will only benefit Thoroughbred Models. Your reputation for excellence and professionalism and the mentoring work you offer to young models, photographers, and creative artists attract me most to your company. It would be an honor to work with you.

Please look at my resume for specific details of my skills, and let's arrange an interview as soon as possible. You won't regret it. Our meeting will not waste your time because I'm honest, I work hard, and . . . I'll come through for you every single day.

Thank you. I eagerly look forward to our meeting . . .

As you write your confidence letter, catch the attention of your reader. Be grounded and authentic in your enthusiasm. Be fearless and creative, and show passion and reason.

18

Mastering the Interview

Finding the humility to happily walk away from those who don't get it unlocks our ability to do good work.

— Seth Godin

Y ou wrote a resume that expresses you. You composed an original and gripping cover letter. Now you've reached the peak of your application journey: the job interview. This is a crucial moment, a culmination of your efforts, and a chance to showcase the unique skills and personality that set you apart. You're not just another candidate; you're an exceptional human being with skills that no one else possesses.

Just like Genevieve...

Genevieve was in her mid to late sixties—professional, elegant, confident, calm, and astute. You knew she was a force to be reckoned with, but one with knowledge, heart, and an abundance of stories you'd be eager to hear.

Still, she was nervous about the interview. She hadn't done one in years and feared she'd be found lacking or simply too old. But she needed to highlight one particular skill.

You see, Genevieve knew Pitman and Gregg shorthand. It was a system used by nearly every secretary—until the Dictaphone and recording devices came on the scene, then it became a lost art, a dinosaur on the brink of extinction. However, since many senior CEOs and directors still liked to give dictation in person, that unusual ability became Genevieve's greatest asset. She maintained the skill because she knew its value. When she dared to share that skill, it allowed her to be booked solid, with the hourly rates she wanted and the option to travel, usually top of the line.

This is what I mean by knowing your skills and your value and building a career that matters at any age. Be like Genevieve.

You, too, have skills. This is a time to relax, be energized, and feel proud of the work you've put in to get here.

I See You, You See Me

Perhaps the fear of rejection raises its ugly head the minute you even think of the word "interview." That's because you're probably viewing it as a Q&A session, where someone sits on the other side of a table and judges you. Instead, think of it as more of a mutual learning experience—a conversation where two people get to know each other.

The word "interview" comes from the French *entrevoir*, which means "to see each other." It's a lovely and moving notion because we all hope to have people genuinely see us and honor the unique value we bring to the table. "I see you. I hear you. You matter."

An interview isn't just an opportunity to be seen and heard but also a chance to discover if an opportunity is the right fit for you. You're evaluating the company and the people you'll potentially work with as much as they are evaluating you. It's not just about impressing them; they need to impress you, too.

Make Friends with Tech

The interviewing process has probably changed since the last time you applied for jobs. This may be one more reason fear could crop up. These days, interviews involve technology, and that's not to be feared but welcomed and enjoyed.

Video conferencing (Zoom, Skype, Microsoft Teams, and GoToMeeting) is friendly and easy to learn. Many YouTube videos can walk you through the process. Take what you learn and practice with friends before attending an interview. Many of the conferencing platforms also offer the ability to hold a "test" call—again, it's all electronic—but it gives you the ability to test your video and sound ahead of time.

Remember, adaptability is an essential skill in today's job market. Learning to quickly master these new interview formats is the first step. It's actually quite exciting when you think about it. This technology allows interviews to take place worldwide, so you don't have to travel to the destination, especially if you will be working remotely. These calls allow you to meet one-on-one or with a few people at a time. So, enjoy the time savings; don't let it stop you from entering the arena.

What to Expect If You Haven't Been on an Interview in a While

Interviews are more holistic now, where your problem-solving skills and cultural company fit are explored, as well as your energy, enthusiasm, empathy, and human skills (as I like to call them, otherwise known as soft skills).

Human skills include listening, caring, offering top service, and going above and beyond to help and get results for people. Interviewers are choosing to surpass the skill set required for the position and are far more focused on your values, vibe, and presence. These are crucial elements.

Choosing the best person for the job is now more meaningful than ever. Employers are less interested in degrees and GPAs when they hire and more in what the person has to offer a company. They're considering you as a person they will work with. They're gauging your life experience, skills, feelings, empathy for others, vulnerability, creativity, commitment, leadership, humility, integrity, and attitude.

Human skills, customer service, teamwork, and problem-solving are highly valued. Be prepared to give an example or two of success you've had in solving a problem or building a project that helped people and was valued by others.

Modern interviewing can also involve evaluating you in unique social settings, such as a restaurant, where people can observe how you communicate, your attitude, listening skills, attention, and what you can contribute. Companies are looking to spot the talent that aligns with their culture, goals, and growth.

The job market is tight, and the assessment process can be stringent. This is not to discourage you; rather, it's to prepare you. Securing a job can take two, three, or four months before an offer is made. Times have changed since we found our jobs in the newspaper classified ads and got a job offer within a week.

Do Your Homework

This new interview timeline is why we discussed researching and becoming deeply curious about job possibilities early on. Select many possibilities. Study the first company, its website, motto, mission statement, history, and the people who work there; then the next. Look especially at the people you are to meet and, more importantly, who you should be meeting. Who are the real decision-makers of the company? Who are the people you must meet? Which people do you desire to work with?

During this drawn-out process, you will encounter brusque people and "brick walls" who refuse to help you. Nonetheless, do all you can to reach the people who will see your assets and back you. Avoid the people who simply check off boxes and follow the steps.

You'll run up against the hiring bullies, the "I don't think out of the box" bully, and HR bullies who could care less about the first word in human resources—human, humanity, people.

Be polite and respectfully go around them to get to the decision-makers. Then decide if this place and people are for you or not.

When something in your research piques your attention, please write it down. Those are the keys, the vital words, and the information about the work team that will help you talk and build rapport during your job interviews. Blend them with who you are and what you do.

Think about it:

- Who are they, this company and people, in the world?
- Who is their competition?
- Where are they in the news?
- How do they make money?
- Where do they stand with social media and technology?
- What are their future goals?
- What is their work culture?
- How do they treat people inside and outside the company?

Write it all down because there will be a point in the interview when you'll be asked, "What questions do you have for me?" You don't want to lead with the number of vacation days or when you'll be promoted. Consciously do deep research. It will enhance your ability to get the job.

Consider the three to six key questions you might ask during the interview. Some examples include:

- What has worked well and created success in the position?
- What do you find missing among the people you are meeting?
- Where are you in the hiring process?
- What change is the company presently working on, and why?
- Who do you respect in business and why?
- What do you like most about your work and the company?

These questions are important because their answers will help you decide if they are a good fit for you.

What to Say About Yourself

Be prepared to discuss your most significant accomplishments because there's a question you can practically bank on being asked in an interview: "Why should I hire you above all the other people I am interviewing?"

People often struggle with this question because they are unprepared. They get caught off guard and are afraid to praise themselves accurately.

That's why you must think of your answer before entering the fray. It builds awareness and confidence. It's deep, logical fun that offers the truth about you. The goal is to eventually get to a one-word answer and then have other words and sentences fill it in, creating rapport between you and the person interviewing you. (I mentioned this narrowing down process in the summary section of the resume-writing chapter. See how the pieces all fit together?)

Here's how to get at that one word...

Exercise: What Do You Do Better Than Anyone Else?

1. Write a paragraph describing "Why Hire You": 200–500 words.

2. Then, edit it into two sentences.

3. Then, refine it into one simple sentence.

4. Finally, select one word.

As an example, we'll use Jamie (whom this exercise inspired). Jamie graduated with a dual major—B.A. in English and Gender, Women's, and Sexuality Studies. She wanted to eventually become a professional writer for TV and films but was looking for entry-level work as a customer service representative, front desk receptionist, and meet-and-greet person in the entertainment field as a jumping-off place.

In the meantime, she worked part-time at an art museum and gave tours. She told stories about art and artists and encouraged others to share their stories. She recognized that this experience would help her in writing jobs, newspaper positions, ghostwriting, editing, etc.

When I asked, "What do you do better than anyone else on the face of the earth?"

She wrote:

"Someone should hire me because I am empathetic. I see the world with a laser focus on how the emotions of others shape their reactions and mine in turn. I want to understand how people feel and evoke honest emotional responses from them. I seek forms of emotional output from myself that allow others to open up to me. I am also tenacious. I seek the answers to problems, even when it's difficult for me to channel my focus onto the problem. I'm curious enough to keep trying. I'm dedicated and passionate about what interests me the most. I'm creative in all aspects of my life. I'm creative at solving my own problems and giving advice to others. I'm creative in my critical thinking and how I view the world as a never-ending story to unfold. I'm creative in that I can create my own stories with no limits to my imagination and no boundaries to what I can portray on the page. I'm a storyteller, which means that I am well-rounded and able to think, invent, entertain, and invest my energy into a product that will tantalize and satisfy people's deepest thoughts and emotions."

From there, Jamie narrowed it down to a few sentences:

> "I should be hired because I delve deeply into the inner workings of other people, valuing emotions above logic. I use my storytelling, creativity, tenaciousness, and empathy skills to guide me toward solving interpersonal problems and allow me to create a unique and new form of structure in any work environment.
>
> "I should be hired because I challenge myself to see my personhood and others through brand-new eyes."

Finally, Jamie landed on her word: **Storyteller!**

I love what she wrote. This is who she truly is—the truth and facts of Jamie.

Tune Into Your Instincts

Follow your instincts as you research and interview. Your brain will be moving fast, connecting you to many things. Keep track of the ideas flooding your mind. They are the touchstones for your interviewing success.

Before any interview, ask yourself the following questions:

- What did they see in my resume and cover letter that made them invite me in to talk?

- How do I fill in the job specifications or description?

- What kind of growth is possible for me here?
- What problem will I solve for them?
- On a scale of 1–10 (1 being low, 10 being high), how much do I want this job?

Trust your instincts; they are your best guide in this process.

How to Dress, What to Carry, and How to Comport Yourself

What to wear for success? It seems simple, even silly, but first impressions are crucial and lasting. Dress professionally. For a man, wear a dark suit and tie; for a casual professional, wear a blazer, pants, and an open-collar shirt. And shine your shoes.

The same goes for a lady: real shoes, not sandals, a pantsuit, or a nice skirt and blouse. If you wear jewelry, make it simple. Be conservative. Be comfortable. Ensure everything fits—not too tight, baggy, revealing, or out-of-date.

And don't leave it until the night before. Decide what to wear while sending out resumes. The goal is to have your skills and personality leave the impression, not your clothing or physical attributes.

With that in mind, here is a quick list of dos and don'ts:

- Don't wear cologne or perfume.
- Take out the hardware—nose, tongue, and eyebrow rings.
- Don't carry a backpack and change in the bathroom.

- Come dressed and pressed.

- Carry a simple briefcase or document envelope to hold your resumes, letters of recommendation, and other essential project work you want to share and leave with the person.

- Bring a pen and a pad of paper for notes. Always be prepared. Ask the interviewer if it is OK for you to jot down some notes. They could say no.

- Have relevant written testimonials from bosses and co-workers to leave with your interviewer. People hardly ever do this. Immediate recognition of your accomplishments builds credibility and motivation for hiring you. Get them to buy into you instantly.

- Ensure you have contacted your references to be prepared to speak with the people interviewing you.

- Make sure emails and telephone numbers are current, as well as the days and times a person is available to talk.

- Have your endorsements printed professionally, formatted, and on good-quality paper. People notice such caring details.

- Bring extra resumes. You never know who you will be meeting.

- Book one interview per day. The process can be lengthy and requires all your attention. Sometimes, you may interview for two to three hours and be asked to return after lunch or at the end of the workday to meet others.

- Be well-groomed—hair, teeth, breath, nails.

- Arrive ten minutes early. Check in and go to the bathroom to check yourself out.

- From the moment you arrive on-site, be courteous and professional to everyone. Don't talk down to the receptionist. They may be interviewing you, and word travels fast about how you treat people.

- Know where you're going. Do a practice run a day or two before your interview. Where is the company located? Will you drive, walk, or take a subway or bus? Is there parking? Is there a security check-in? Time of day is key; morning is busy as people commute. It's better to be early and calm than frantic. Same with lunchtime and going home. Don't risk being late, getting lost, or panicky. You're stepping into a new environment, offices, and people you have not experienced. Arriving early helps you adapt and soak it all in.

- Turn off your phone and don't text. Be fully present as you wait.

- Get a good night's sleep and do whatever focuses and relaxes you in the morning. Eat breakfast, exercise, meditate, or play your favorite music to power up and settle in. Don't rush around. Be positive.

- Breathe deeply, stand up, and confidently shake hands when you meet your interviewer. Make sure your handshake is firm and dry. Call them by name and have their bio clearly in mind.

- Smile, talk to the person, and make eye contact. Watch your posture. Don't slump or fold your arms.

- Be ready to discuss your achievements, why you want the job, how you solved a tough problem, and your weaknesses and strengths.

- Answer the questions honestly and be your true self. That's how you win.

- Don't make jokes or ramble on. Don't talk against people—no complaining, whining, or negativity.

- Understandably, you'll be a bit nervous, but avoid using too many fillers, buzzwords, and phrases such as: "cool, awesome, uh, uh, uh, like, like, like, innovative, track record, extensive knowledge, communication skills, problem solver, think on my feet..."

- Be direct and have succinct examples to support your work and accomplishments.

Above all, enjoy the process. Answer the questions honestly and be your true self. That's how you win.

Follow Up

It's important to say thank you and ask for a personal business card when the interview ends. All the information you will need to follow up is there. Do this with everyone you meet. "How may I keep in touch with you?" It's the question to ask at the conclusion of the interview. Should I email you or call? The person will tell you. They may like email or prefer you call their assistant. They may give you a specific time of day: early morning or never after five p.m.

You may ask how soon they want to fill the position or where they are in the hiring process.

When you leave, thank the receptionist. Get their name because they will help you reach the people with whom you met.

When you exit, head to a coffee shop and write down your impressions. Where did things go well? Where could you have done better? Then, write thank-you notes to everyone—a different and original note for each person. Don't be generic; send it immediately by mail or by email within twenty-four hours. PROOFREAD IT. Ensure you use the right words: "effect/affect... to/too...compliment/complement...who/whom...personnel/personal." Show it to people with good editing skills who know you and your style.

You want them to know how grateful you are for their time and your interest in the job. Gratitude is a powerful strength. It's also memorable and attractive to others.

If a week or more passes without hearing, follow up via phone or email. Be friendly; simply check in to see if any decisions have been made and express your continued enthusiasm for working for them.

What if They Say No

I want to encourage you to be innovative, ask for what you want, think outside the box, and have a plan A, B, C, right down to X, Y, and Z. Don't simply accept no. Be bold and take a risk.

If they are hesitant to hire you or say no, why not ask them to give you a try? Temp you for one or two weeks to see how you work. Let them see how you fit in and stand out with the team.

Ask them to give you a project to create or a problem to solve in two days.

If they want to hire you and the salary is too low, be direct and negotiate. For example, you might say, "If I increase your client base and raise your sales number to this number in three months, then raise my salary to this. If I continue in another three months with equal, if not better, results, then raise my salary to this." This way, you gain back the level of salary you desire, and you also show your worth. (If they agree, make sure you get it in writing.)

Confidence and creativity. Be professionally aggressive. Show your business acumen. All they can say is no, and you're prepared for rejection and success.

Mentern = Mentor + Intern

If you're a mature person, you will most likely meet people from different generations who may have some preconceptions about you as you interview. As I've mentioned before, ageism is real, and you should be aware of what you may encounter in interviews so you can adjust your approach and tactics to connect with everyone in the best way possible.

Which leads me to the positive and pleasing idea of "menterns." Entrepreneur and hotelier Chip Conley first created the concept of a mentern—someone willing to share their expertise with others (mentor) while learning something new (intern). In other words, you can sell the benefit of your mentern-ing for a company because you bring a generational skill set and approach that may be missing from the workplace.

A mentern plays a crucial role in bridging the gap between Baby Boomers and Millennials. The unique blend of mentoring and interning is a powerful tool in fostering understanding and collaboration across all generations.

Understanding the six sets of people in the workforce today is key to your ability to mentern; they include:

1. Modern sages born before or around 1945

2. Baby Boomers,

   1945–1964

3. Generation X,

   1965–1980

4. Gen Y's,

   1981–1995

5. Gen Z,

   1996–2009

6. Generation Alpha,

   2010–2024

Each generation has different work experience, expectations, technological knowledge, and communication styles. As the six generations connect and work together, there can be clashes. You can help bridge those clashes, which, if you ask me, is a real selling point.

Final Thoughts

Every interview should promote your integrity, worth, pride, and gratitude. Keep going after the jobs you want. Apply and interview until you get it. It's your dream, your future, and your success. You should be happy at work.

Interviews are an opportunity; they're an adventure to talk, listen, and ask questions. They are a chance to learn more about an open position, company, and the people you might work with to see if they're right for you.

Be clear about why you are the right person for the job.

Remember to have answers:

- What do I do better than anyone else on the face of the earth?

- Why should a company hire me out of all the other people applying?

Show yourself in your interviews until someone sees you and your value and knows you are the best person for the job—and the right person to join the team.

19

How to Create a Job from Thin Air

———

Everyone has been made for some particular work,
and the desire for that work has been put in every heart.

—Rumi

This is where some people fall down on the job. They wait in their current holding pattern until they see something jump out from the shadows and hit them square in the nose. "Here I am, your next fabulous job!" I say, go out and create your next opportunity. Which is where this story comes in.

Whenever I needed to make money, I didn't wait around for my next big break to drop in my lap; I asked people to help me find work. As if by magic, something always came up on a temporary basis. I cleaned apartments, worked in a bookstore, catered and waited on tables, delivered subpoenas, attended focus groups, shopped for groceries, delivered dry cleaning, and performed singing telegrams. I cared, showed my worth, showed up happy, and offered solid service, and things happened—as they will for you.

A temporary gig may not look exactly like what you're going for, but get in, and you'll have the chance to look around and see a potential opening for you. You could create opportunities to stay and grow, especially if you like the people, the company, or the work.

For instance, I was set up to clean out a large storage room at an international Greek tourist cruise company at Rockefeller Center. The job didn't sound glamorous, but when I got there, it was even worse than I had imagined. The place looked like a tornado had hit it. The room was where the company dumped stuff they didn't care about and had no place to store. The thing is, I'm a superb organizer, so this was an incredible opportunity for me. I went to work; about three weeks later, the place looked like the New York Public Library.

The art director was impressed and arranged for me to keep working for them. I answered phones, then moved to the mail room to package brochures, stock shelves, and learn about the mail system. I also learned how to telex the three ships they owned whenever they needed answers for clients traveling with special requests.

I really wanted to learn how to book cruises and work with customers. So, one night, after most people had gone home, I went to the head of customer service and asked if he had an opening in sales. He handed me a telephone number and the name of a prospective person to call and see how I handled myself.

So, I did. The person didn't want to book a cruise and nearly hung up, but I wouldn't let him off the phone because this was my chance to prove myself. I asked the man, "If you could travel with us to Venice or the Greek islands, the Orinoco River, or do a transatlantic crossing, which destination would you choose?"

He told me Venice, and we talked about why; eventually, I discovered that in less than six months, he would be celebrating his wedding anniversary. What an opening. "Why don't you let me send you our brochure, and in one week, I'll call you back; if you like what you see and what I have to say, we can give you an option on a seven- or fourteen-day cruise from Venice to Nice for you and your wife. What a surprise for her." He agreed.

The head of customer service hired me immediately. And yes, the man booked the cruise.

I ended up staying in customer service for several years, booking cruises, air reservations, and hotels. I also helped develop a booking process for top executives from various companies.

This was a choice opportunity that was initially dressed in rags. The company was highly successful, and the people were friendly and professional. It was located in a great place, and the pay and benefits were excellent.

If you need to make money fast, take whatever work you can and see what it can be. Think about it for a minute:

- What are the possibilities for you?
- What job can you create for yourself inside the company?
- What might a company be missing?

- Where can you fill a gap?
- What relationships can you build?

Speaking of relationships, when working for the cruise company, the owner's wife took a liking to me. She was hardworking and had no problem rolling up her sleeves and pitching in. She asked my opinion about their brochures, what clients wanted, and how they could improve. I told her. She used to call me from Greece to follow up, and we would work closely on growing the customer service for their cruises. That relationship allowed me to become indispensable, and it also helped me satisfy my creative bent. Win-win.

Even if a temporary job isn't exactly what you'd like, you must always knock people out with genuine care and exceptional service and go above and beyond what is expected. Make yourself indispensable. Show all your skills and ambition. Put your heart and soul into it. Speak up if you want something more. Be innovative. Work well with others. And see what opportunities arise.

Create Through Relationship

Going out and engaging with strangers can be the best way to drum up opportunities. Network wherever you can—with people you know, within your local community—and build relationships with those you meet in whatever venue.

Yes, this could mean stopping at a meet and greet of the local Chamber of Commerce, but you could have a lot more fun than that. For instance, I recently read a book I loved; I was so impressed and grateful that I looked up the author on LinkedIn, sent him my impressions, and asked if I could add him to my connections on LinkedIn. We connected and are having some great conversations.

This is what I call spotting and creating opportunities and building relationships that could benefit you as you search for work and build business. How many people could you sincerely connect with per day after researching them? This goes far beyond following or liking someone on social media.

Here's another example to get your ideas churning (particularly if you can't imagine doing this)...

In my coaching work, I encourage people to network and build relationships with as many people as possible as they look for work and promote their own work. The idea is to allow for sudden inspiration to hit you after you've read something, watched a video, or heard an interview that compels you to connect with the creator or subject somehow.

And I believe in leading by example. Here's an email I sent to Arianna Huffington on May 3, 2014, which enabled me to become a HuffPost Blogger, something I dreamed about.

"Hello, Arianna,

We have never met, but I am a great admirer of your work. You give me strength and new things to think about.

I watched you talk at Google. It was fantastic and very emotional to hear you speak of your accident and the new choices you made and continue to discover as you change your life and 'THRIVE.'

I especially like how you talk about people. You show people such respect.

I also like how you care for yourself with sleep. It's so essential for creativity, clarity, and exciting peace in our lives.

I'm an avid reader of the Huffington Post and share many of your articles with my clients and social networks. I just wanted to connect with you and express my gratitude for the deep and good effect you have on me.

Continued happiness on your joyful and brave journey.

My very best,

Michael Feeley: Life, Career, and Change Coach"

Here is her reply of May 4, 2014:

"Michael, thank you so much for the kind note. I enjoyed the Google Hangout and would love to continue the conversation on HuffPost about how you are redefining success in your own life. I'm cc'ing our blog editor so you can send her a post, photo, and bio.

All the best,

Arianna."

I immediately followed up with the blog editor after the article was published, and sure enough, Arianna sent me another email.

She wrote:

> "Many thanks, Michael. Please continue contributing to HuffPost!
>   Warmly,
>   Arianna."

I wrote many articles for them, which helped me grow my coaching business, skills, and writing reputation.

Think about it. With whom and how might you open the door for a business relationship? Once you have a person in mind, take the steps to get in touch. (With respect and gratitude, in a non-threatening way, mind you.)

Ask for Help and Time

We learn early on not to ask for things, not to show our emotions, to act cool and removed, and to appear as though we have it all together. Yet you need to learn to go after what you want with fervor and heart and not stop—because it matters. Yes, some will say no. But keep asking. It's far better than hiding and sabotaging your dreams or kicking yourself for missing a chance because you were too much of a coward, too arrogant, and/or felt too undeserving to ask.

"I need your help" has a way of opening doors. (Have you spotted the ask-for-help theme yet? Well, you should.) Reach out to people you know and tell them you're looking for work and could use their help. Set up a time to discuss your work and brainstorm with them.

People want to help, and a community is usually willing to provide support and encouragement. Why go it alone? Become an encourager in those helpful communities. It's one of the most rewarding jobs you can ever have. You can help others, which is satisfying, and they can help you.

Along the same lines as asking for what you want, don't be afraid to contact people you specifically want to work with...

There was one voice teacher I was desperate to study with. I got her number from one of her students and called to see if I could audition and work with her. She told me she was booked solid and not taking on any new students. So, I said, "Please let me sing for you; if you like what you hear, you could put me on your waitlist, and when there's an opening, we can start singing together."

"I like that," she said. "You didn't take no for an answer."

We set up a time, I sang one song, and she said, "How could I not work with someone who sings with that kind of passion?"

We started working together. What an honor.

Asking for what you want is more than a simple request; it's a powerful tool that creates opportunity. (Think: Tool, not Rule.) When you see a desirable possibility, why not do all you can to get it? We're all afraid of failure to some degree or another, which is part of being human. But even if you fail, you tried, and that's something to be proud of. It's about the courage to ask, the belief in your worth, and the readiness to accept the outcome.

It's also about the approach. Ask with respect, confidence, and gratitude, and then be ready to produce. Acknowledge the other person's position while believing in your worth, and express appreciation for the opportunity, even if it is unclear if one exists.

Put on a Show

Sometimes, asking for an opportunity doesn't involve reaching out to a particular person or gatekeeper, but acting without obvious approval. Think of this as freely sharing your talents and skills with the world or a specific audience.

Here are a few examples that illustrate this step:

Get up and sing wherever you can and often.
Paint and hang up your art where there is an open space.
Write and publish daily.
Put your tap shoes on and make noise to be known.
Plumber away. Taxi away. Video away. Tailor away. Bed and Breakfast away. Cook, clean, and service like no one else.

Practice and condition yourself to be ready at a moment's notice. Expect the spotlights to go on and to take center stage. Be alert and aware of opportunities to share your skills and knowledge with others.

Case in Point: Early in my career placing freelancers, a woman named Vanessa unexpectedly stopped by my office to talk. She was polished, articulate, and so nice to talk to. She told me she had registered with the company some time ago but had never been called for work. With great confidence, she expressed her excellent skills as an executive assistant and asked that we please try her. She guaranteed she would not let me down. I looked up her application, and she seemed wonderful. I told her to be dressed in the mornings and ready to go; I would try her out as soon as I had a temp opening.

Not long afterward, a one-day temp job opened on the executive floor of a prominent financial client, and I sent her in. When my boss learned of my choice, she ripped me apart for sending a person they had never used. She called the client and apologized, but the client said she would keep her for the day.

Well, they loved Vanessa, and the CEO wanted her there indefinitely to replace the current person. Eventually, he hired her permanently. I was thrilled for her! She was exactly what she said she was and more. She took a risk and stepped forward, asking for help, having guts and self-pride. She made things happen.

You have something vital to offer. Prove it. Harness inspiration and interest, build momentum, and go after what you want. Build the right conditions, then vote yourself in. That is a big part of creating your opportunities.

Go Where the Work Is

You must seek out the people, audience, customers, and clients you were born to serve. It's about being proactive and engaging in your professional growth, not waiting for opportunities to come to you.

Where could you go to create opportunity? Think for just a minute to allow your imagination to engage...

If you're a yoga teacher, for example, you could head to the community library and arrange to teach a class there. Then, you could let people know who you are, what you do, and where they can find you.

To help spread the word about your services, you could get an interview with the local newspaper, TV, or radio station. You could also go to schools, universities, gyms, churches, hospitals, and assisted living communities and fervently encourage people to hire you. It's about being persistent, determined, and focused on seeking the opportunities you deserve.

Create a business card and hand out two at a time, one for the person you want to attract and one for a friend of theirs.

Hang up fliers in coffee shops or your local go-to spot. Spread the news about *you.* You need to market yourself. Be resilient and committed to your goals. Don't give up when faced with challenges.

Wow Them Where You Are

Let's go back to the idea that you can create opportunities where you are by performing in a refreshed, vibrant manner.

Do your work even when you think you can't (and don't want to). Try and keep trying. Lead, step by step, into solutions and create awe. In other words, perform; don't simply go through the motions because you never know who is watching. Stun people. Leave them wanting more and raving about their trust and love for you, your services, and your product.

Find a pattern, a method, a plan, a strategy, and put yourself out there. Give people what they want and more because they are looking for you and what you offer.

Be Your Own Champion

Figure out who you are, what you want, and why. You're a professional. Be the champion of your life: show up, train, do your best, and give your all. Do it at fifty, sixty, seventy, eighty, and beyond. Do all you can to make your life meaningful and magical so you can honestly say, "I love my life and my work."

It all goes back to the POA and the motivation required to overcome resistance. Since I am a career coach, and I truly want you to succeed, here are some individual thoughts that may help you along the way:

- Obtaining what you want requires guts, logic, data, and facts—it also takes love, a big dash of magic, and getting yourself to the right place at the right time.

- Your dreams become reality because you've forged a strong, unbreakable bond with the possibility of their achievement. Hold onto this belief with unwavering faith; let it fuel your determination to make your dreams a reality.

- Intention goes with creating opportunities. It takes a wish to the next level by aligning your thoughts, feelings, and actions toward your goal and staying focused on it despite any challenges or distractions that may come your way.

- Creating and earning an opportunity is based on believing the world will come through for you. Trust the world, and you trust yourself at the same time. It's a beautiful blend.

- There is enough opportunity for everyone. All you need to do is look; when you see the opportunity, you should take it. Go and introduce yourself to the chance.

- Opportunity is a specific time or circumstance that comes your way when you are ready to step into the life you dream about and, hopefully, have been actively working to achieve.

- Don't allow resistance to stop you from embracing your opportunity; refuse to listen to the fear or lie that you don't deserve it or that you're not up to the challenge.

- When opportunity knocks, say yes with an open heart. Leap in. Take the risk.

- It's a bit like a voyage—discovering who you are, living as you please (without harm to others), looking for opportunities to learn, grow, and change. Sometimes, it's smooth sailing; other times, it's stormy, rough seas where you're just trying to stay afloat.

- The word "opportunity" was once a term used by sailors to mean "coming toward a port." Sailors are always looking for the opportunity of a favorable, good wind to steer their ship to a safe harbor.

- Any journey will change you if you let it. That's why we travel: to discover and connect with new places, people, and things and come home refreshed, improved, and more ourselves.

- Time is precious, so take every opportunity—create it if you must—and live your life full-out; make it count.

Conclusion

Tell me, what is it you plan to do with your one wild and precious life?
—Mary Oliver

I'd like to tell you a story about one of my clients. It's the
story of a man who yearned to work at something he genuinely cared about, that inspired him every day and ulti-
mately benefited others. He was beyond bored and had lost all
hope for a brighter professional future. The motivation necessary to make a change was, how shall we say it, missing in action.
Until something woke him up.

Mark reached out to me for help finding a new job because
he was miserable. (I would put miserable in all caps, but my editor would scold me.) He wrote, "I wake up in the morning and
have a physical destination to go to, but it is nothing more than
that. I would love to use my day more substantively, where my
energies could be applied to a larger goal or vision with motive
and passion."

Mark had worked at the same place for over fifteen years and
was going nowhere. He felt as though he was wasting away doing
the same thing day after day after day. Like many peo-

ple, he didn't know what he wanted to do and wasn't sure how to figure that out.

He found it challenging to overcome the personal roadblocks he encountered during his job search. (By now, you know all about them.) He often felt discouraged, quickly finding reasons why he was not qualified and fearing he wouldn't be able to succeed in a new job. With the right guidance and support, of course, he was able to break through these barriers, a process that brought him relief and a sense of empowerment.

I don't have to remind you that we all limit ourselves with fears and self-doubt when we think about change. But Mark's choice of a fresh start with a new job propelled him to face his gremlins head-on. He wanted a change. It's true for any of us—change will only happen when we want to change and find our present circumstances unbearable. The key is personal motivation, which can lift us up and forward to make the changes we desire.

Mark was highly successful at what he did. He was a decision-maker at an established financial firm, handling large amounts of money, liaising with top directors and influential clients, and supplying excellent customer service. He was trusted, counted on, and respected for his abilities and his mind. He consistently met deadlines and was creative, fun, and a valued employee. What company wouldn't want him?

It was nearly impossible for Mark to see this because he was heartbreakingly unhappy and self-defeating. He was articulate but unable to speak, nearly lifeless. His personal bully told him,

"You'll never succeed. You're stuck for good. There's no way out for you."

Mark had taken a job to make a living and bring value to other people and the world. He began with a deep and honest hope of doing his best work. He wanted to grow and be acknowledged and appreciated for his abilities and successes. But this didn't happen, so he fell back into a daily routine of just showing up and not being fully present. Perhaps you can relate. It's easy, but it's a quiet agony that sucks the life out of you. And the older you get, the harder it is to pull out of the death spiral.

Staying in a dead-end job out of comfort will cause anger and deep personal disappointment because you're not truly engaged with who you are and not living up to your potential. You're missing out on daily wonders and opportunities to change and transform yourself and others, to be new, powerful, original, creative, generous, and make contributions to your job.

It takes brave work to know and understand yourself and find out why you're in your situation. It's not impossible or hopeless because the answers are in you, waiting to be released.

Mark began to recognize how much he had accented the negative and defaulted to putting himself down, feeling he would not amount to much. He could see that he was run by resistance, harshly limiting himself, but he was learning how to make new and better choices, to shift his low energy of anger and apathy, and to reframe things in a far more positive way.

What helped him most was sticking to the facts: what was true in his life and work, who he was, his gifts, knowledge, and skills—his authentic value. This allowed him to see the importance of what he did in his present job, his significant worth to himself, and the firm he worked for. He saw that these were transferable to many other jobs and companies.

Finally, he was able to actively respect and love himself unconditionally with dignity, wonder, pride, and heartfelt gratitude. He was breathing new life into himself and his work.

Knowing the truth about yourself is a liberating and inspiring experience.

Mark enthusiastically spoke about a job listing that interested him and made him think differently about seeking new work. He began to work on his resume and cover letter, asked questions about interviews and salary negotiations, and created a profile on LinkedIn.

From there, he achieved new results, saw how resourceful he could be, and grew as he researched companies to work for and thought about new possibilities in fields he loved, such as writing, music, entertainment, and research.

Mark loved music—going to concerts, listening, and researching. He knew he wasn't meant to perform but decided he'd like to be close to it. We studied people who made a living in music, not just the few lucky ones but teachers, singers, and musicians who worked in churches and performed at events—any place where they were expressed while making money. We created visioning exercises on where he'd like to work, the business culture of companies, the daily routine of his next job, and many other details.

Mark began to see that his skills, aptitude, and love for numbers, customer service, accuracy, and professionalism could also be applied to the creative world: industries related to music, publishing, concert halls, and recording artists. All could utilize his skills and enable him to make a living while allowing him to remain close to his love for music. If he wanted to and was willing to try, he could create opportunities and ask for what he wanted because it mattered to him.

So, Mark sent out three resumes for music-related jobs each week.

He discovered how much he had wanted and needed music throughout his life and saw no reason he couldn't have it daily in his work.

Mark worked hard to know himself and what he wanted, to break up the blocks that stopped him from being whole and happy. Take note: as you release blocks, you, too, can create an openness for new possibilities and learning. You, too, can gain greater clarity and move closer to what you desire for your life. You, too, can act and learn to welcome change.

Mark once wrote, "I have come to appreciate that self-perception is a real, tangible thing that can either drive you to great heights or steer you right off a cliff into a bottomless abyss . . . the power of positive thinking, along with due diligence, has the power to strengthen your mind and core for nearly any adventure. I'm giving what I feel and what I want a chance. I'm taking steps to get out of myself and to leave a bad work situation.

I'm stretching myself beyond my familiar thoughts and ways of doing things."

Stretching beyond the familiar inspired Mark to build a resume he loved, where once the idea of writing one had crippled him. He discovered that his great love of music could be part of his new job. He set up a blog and wrote about music, performers, and concerts to attract opportunities. He continued to steadily send out resumes and cover letters to music-related companies and jobs he'd carefully researched.

All of this happened because he dared to try new things, dream, and live his best life because he saw the tangible possibility of his hopes.

Mark pursued a realistic dream, and in the process, he discovered new things about himself. He was an exacting man, measured and careful about facts, with a great sense of humor, kindness, and new possibilities and options. He also learned to listen to his heart—to live with passion—and this was fairly new territory for him to travel in. He was exploring himself and the outside world, which gave him such profound and sincere pleasure, comfort, ease, peace, and joy.

We make choices to either honor ourselves or knock ourselves down, to see things positively or negatively, and we pay for those choices by living with gratitude, hope, and happiness, or fear and despair.

You're on the road to true happiness and success when you find what you want to do with your life. Why should you live any other way?

Your Journey Forward

This is not the end but the exciting beginning of a journey towards profound emotional and tangible change. As you read, think, and identify yourself here, you are already living this transformation.

Whether you are 50, 60, 70, or 80, I invite you to recognize your worth and the wealth of knowledge you possess. You are relevant. You matter. Your years do not limit you; they empower you, and you have the potential to make more significant contributions to the world until reality says, "Time's up."

With all my heart, I hope you see and feel the value of who you are and what you do. The intense value of your skills—knowing they are transferable to any other job or career you choose. Your abilities, gifts, talents, credentials, knowledge, life experiences, core values, connections, collaborations, successes, and even failures matter. Your skills are not just valuable; they are exceptional and indispensable, and they are the foundation upon which you can build a new and fulfilling career. You have put your whole life into your skills with the work that you've done, all of it.

Whether you've already identified your desires and goals or are still on the path of self-discovery, it's important to remember your potential for growth. You have the needs, wants, drive, and tools to continue learning about yourself and to make a difference with your presence.

You may choose to stay in your current job and renew and reinvent yourself. It's highly possible, and you will surprise and encourage others around you as you do, giving them permission to also shine and be all they can be.

You may decide to move to a different company and do similar work. What's familiar, yet new and different, can open doors and instill momentum.

You may leap into building a brand-new career because this is what you want, and you trust yourself and the world. You trust other people to help you. You must believe the world has your back and is creating your success because it does, and it is. You are not alone on this journey. A network of support and resources is available to you, ready to guide you and help you succeed. With this support, you can confidently step into a new stage of your life, your encore.

You've asked yourself the tough questions:

- What do I want?
- What are the truth and the facts about me and my work?
- How can I better live by these truths and facts?
- What do I do better than anyone else on the earth?
- What is my detailed, realistic vision for change, happiness, and success?
- How will I face my fears and doubts with understanding and compassion?
- What does it mean to practice living my best life?
- How can I create and spot opportunities?
- When will I ask for what I want?

- What does it mean for me to be a professional?

Now, never give up on your dreams. They never give up on you. You always have a choice.

Just think of the unlikely path I took . . .

At forty-five, I stopped a long-acting and singing career I loved. I went after reinventing myself in the service of finding people jobs.

My career as a headhunter abruptly ended at age fifty-eight. After a soul-searching break and rejuvenation period, I went back to school and became a certified life and career coach.

For the past fifteen years, I've built my own business and worked for myself.

At sixty, I moved to a Caribbean island to live the quality of life that mattered to me, one filled with peace, joy, and love.

At sixty-two, I opened my own real estate company, continued to coach people, and applied all my skills to helping people find a home in the world and within themselves.

At seventy, I was hired as a coach for Seth Godin's Akimbo, The Creative's Workshop (TCW). It was a dream come true and the pinnacle of my coaching career.

At seventy-two, I wrote this book to express my authority and help other people like you find their value. Because I am not done yet, and neither are you.

You get one life, and you should live it exceptionally well. There are no reruns or returns. The quality of the life you choose to lead is up to you, so make it real and worthwhile. Your choices make your life. Choose to do the work you love, work you're proud of, and work that makes a difference for others and the world.

You were placed on this earth to do important work. You, my friend, are wild and precious. You can get it done.

Bon Voyage!

Acknowledgments

Writing about my life stirs up gratitude for the people and events that have made it count. Although I have never met some of them, their work has influenced and changed my life for the better.

Seth Godin inspired me to write this book because "books are persistent." Nobody challenges me more or has more goodwill for me than he does.

Ann Sheybani, a masterful editor and publisher, showed up when I needed the lights turned on and stayed with me throughout the book-writing journey. She saw one sentence, one idea, which blossomed into this book.

I thank the team at Summit Press Publishers, including Amy Barton for her copyediting skills and heart, and Ahmed "Maddy" Raza for his generous and innovative book cover designs. Walt Hampton, thank you for your marketing wisdom. Melissa Kascak, thank you for chopping wood and carrying water for everyone.

Arianna Huffington enabled me to become a Huffington Post blogger—a dream come true.

Michael Port, thank you for asking me to write a blog post for your website, which began my writing career.

Kristin Hatcher, without you, there would be no Akimbo WIC—Writing in Community. Thank you and all my cohorts who supported me in countless ways in creating this book.

My gratitude goes to Dr. Terence Maltbia of Columbia University, who gave me two hours of his valuable time on Christmas Eve to answer questions about coaching.

Chip Conley, thank you for always showing up, producing, and giving without limit.

To TCW—The Creative's Workshop—and the 8 a.m. Monday Morning Goose Gathering Group: Paula Braun, Angela Beeching, Domenic Chiarella, Michael Reilly, and Cece Schweitzer.

To the Writing in Community (WIC) 4:30 p.m. Monday Zoom Egret Group: Kathy Karn and her beloved elephants, Nicolette Wills, and Dr. Cynthia Miller.

To Scott Perry for his years of happiness, creative support, and leadership in all the Akimbo Workshops.

Louise Karch, you are a guardian angel with humor, eagle eyes, and a kind, open heart. Thank you for supporting this book in unlimited ways.

Andrew Ingkavet, thank you for your trust in my work. Roel Bello, Vic S., Mary Susan Burns Hoff, Sana Fayyaz, Laura Millman Meagher, Diana Simion, Julio Baptista Barroco, and Lillian Mahoukou.

You, Tom Huntington, a technical and emotional lifeguard, came to my rescue one night when I was lost in computer land.

To Alford Wayman, an artist with kindness and strength; Lizette Kelly and Veena Grover for your consistent yoga spirit;

Pegret Harrison for your belief in my words; and Esther Blanche Scheidler for years of support.

Julien Fortuit for steady, generous encouragement and endless creativity.

Dr. Nadine Kelly for deep friendship, steady inspiration, and a wise heart.

Lisa Marie Dias for media expertise, friendship, and insistence that I consistently write a blog.

Dr. Martha Beck, your book *Finding Your Own North Star* changed the direction of my life.

Thank you, Oprah Winfrey, for triggering new emotions I didn't know existed.

Bernadette Jiwa, thank you for your fabulous Story Skills Workshop.

Byron Katie, Deepak Chopra, Anthony William, Kelly Brogan, M.D., Adam Grant, and Michael Bungay Stanier for your coaching expertise; Susan Scott for your company, Fierce Inc., and for answering my inquiries about your work.

Steven Pressfield for your true vision of Resistance in *The War of Art*, and Natalie Goldberg for what you taught me about writing in your glorious book *Writing Down the Bones*.

Shakespeare, Sondheim, Oscar Wilde, Chekhov, Chopin, Verdi, Mozart, Marilyn Horn, Ruth Ann Swensen.

Margaret McElroy and Sally Ann Walsh—my speech and drama coaches from elementary to high school; Elizabeth Joselyn, Judy and Neil Person; Sister Anna Louise for your humor and music; Sister Patricia Gertrude and Sister Ronan.

Church organist Mary Ward for hearing the gift of singing that I did not hear from myself; Alice and Dr. Ben Duffy, Kate Duffy, Betty and Frank Feeley, Aunt Betty, and Aunt Mary.

Cantor Arthur Koret—a generous voice teacher; Frank Hakenson; Maria Weida—an acting teacher who cared; Edward Greer; Herman Reutter, Dean Emeritus Stuttgart Academy of Music; the actress Sara Croft; Maria Farnworth—another voice teacher goddess; Michael Thomas, a gentleman of an agent; Miller Wright, one more guardian angel; Phyllis Grandy—a phenomenal accompanist; and the poet and philosopher Eli Siegel, who taught me what it means to like the world.

Joel Zwick—who heard my song and made my dream come true as a professional actor and singer in New York City; Yolanda Roca—a loving friend; John Raitt, Howard Keel, Joanna Merlin, Hal Prince; Anne-Marie Cullinane—a natural and longtime friend; Jim Cahill and Roger Bailey... always in my heart; Deborah Van der Grift, Bruce Schneider, Johanna and Wim Schutten for your generous friendship and great humor. Tulla—our beloved Yorkie companion for thirteen years, and Al—for endless love, happiness, and integrity.

About The Author

MICHAEL FEELEY was a professional actor in New York City and then a headhunter. He's been a career and life coach, assisting people worldwide in creating the change they desire, and a coach in Seth Godin's online Akimbo Workshop – The Creative's Workshop. He writes and publishes daily on his blog, Commit2Change. Like Prospero in Shakespeare's play *The Tempest*, he lives on a Caribbean island surrounded by beauty and magic. He sees himself as vintage . . . only getting better with age. You can connect with Michael by email: MF@michaelfeeleylifecoach.com

BONUS

Tired of feeling stuck in a job that no longer feeds your soul? Hesitant to make a change because you're "too old" ... not to mention afraid? Time to own your transferable skills, master your mindset, and set yourself up for job success. Better yet, it's time to access the additional free resources I've mentioned throughout the book. Head on over to michaelfeeleylifecoach.com/bonus

www.ingramcontent.com/pod-product-compliance
Lightning Source LLC
Chambersburg PA
CBHW062054080426
42734CB00012B/2641